# MENTORING FOR FUTURE KINGS AND QUEENS

## YOUR MISSION...
## IF YOU CHOOSE TO ACCEPT IT?

## J. A. JUBILEE
## &
## T. J. FAULK

Copyright © 2017 by T.J. Faulk

Mentoring For Future Kings and Queens
By T. J. Faulk

All rights reserved solely by the author. The author guarantees all contents are original and do not infringe upon the legal rights of any other person or work. This book or any portion thereof may not be reproduced or used in any manner whatsoever without the express written permission of the author except for the use of brief quotations in a book review. All references, credits, and quotes identified are used for spiritual review, analysis, and education.

Unless otherwise indicated, Bible quotations come from Bible.org, BibleGateway.com then validated against the Parallel Study Bible - New International Version & King James Version of the Bible. Copyright © 2013, by Zondervan.

Printed in the United States of America

First Printing, Oct 20, 2017

ISBN 978-164136295-5

Up High Publishing
Powder Springs, GA 30127


TJFJ20@uphighpublishing.com

# Reviews

T.J. Faulk brings a wealth of information, inspiration, and motivation in an easy to read package that will appeal to anyone looking for answers to life's questions for an effective, successful, path to maturation in today's culture. I'm not just saying this because he is a brilliant, soft spoken, Christian gentleman, that I am privileged to call friend and colleague or because he honored me by acknowledging me by name among giants of nationally and internationally renowned scholars and theologians; but because it is penned for all ages to comprehend. Fortunately, I have the same Christian values and world view that is evident in his content making it easy for me to read without dissension but with full affirmation.

Minister Phil Phinisee Sr.

A divine and timely "How to" guide for our youth, mentors, and anyone that may be starting their walk in establishing a relationship with God. The book is laid out in a manner that eliminates any gray areas or ambiguity with what God's expectations are for us as it pertains to his word. The examples provided for each lesson are easy to understand and relevant to today's society.

Some of my favorite pearls of wisdom shared in the book come from chapter 16 which is entitled "Can't is a Curse Word." T.J. highlights the importance of removing the word can't from your vocabulary, staying positive in challenging times, staying away from negativity, increasing the number of compliments vs complaints, and choosing your battles wisely. Reading this chapter gave me a burst of energy and a renewed sense of purpose as I face the day to day challenges of life.

As much as the world promotes quick and easy is the way to go, this special treasure should be taken in doses. There is a lot of wisdom being shared in each chapter so I would recommend taking a chapter or two at a time. T.J Faulk gives a thorough assessment and application of God's word or fruit that will nourish the spirit, mind, and body while paving our road to success. Simply stated, <u>Mentoring for Future Kings & Queens: Your Mission..If you choose to accept it?</u> By T.J. Faulk is the Mr. Miyagi to the young Daniels of the world. Greatly needed and critical in the success of our future King and Queens.

Jamila Ramsay M.B.A

# Table of Content

| | |
|---|---|
| Dedication | vii |
| Acknowledgments | ix |
| Prologue | xiii |
| Letter to Readers | xv |

## Fruit for the Spirit

| | | |
|---|---|---|
| 1. | Your Mission (Question) | 1 |
| 2. | Where Do I Start | 3 |
| 3. | Rules of Engagement | 11 |
| 4. | Things God Despises | 23 |
| 5. | Free Will – God's Gift | 35 |
| 6. | Sacrifice and Salvation | 43 |
| 7. | Is Your Heart Aligned with Heaven or Hell | 59 |
| 8. | Dark Forces | 67 |
| 9. | Know Your Armor – Now Put It On | 73 |
| 10. | Art and Science of Forgiveness | 77 |

## Fruit for the Mind and Body

| | | |
|---|---|---|
| 11. | Parent and Child Fellowship | 81 |
| 12. | Your Temple | 89 |
| 13. | The difference "Between" An Adult and A Child | 93 |
| 14. | Taboo of Idleness | 97 |
| 15. | Life Is No Music Video | 103 |

# Fruit for Success

| | |
|---|---|
| 16. Can't Is A Curse Word | 107 |
| 17. School | 111 |
| 18. After High School | 121 |
| 19. Your Future - Career and Goals | 125 |
| 20. Intelligent Investments | 141 |
| 21. Life's Storms | 147 |
| 22. Your Mission (Answer) | 153 |
| | |
| Reading Suggestions | 157 |
| About the Author | 161 |
| Chess Pieces on the Cover | 163 |
| References and Credits | 165 |

# DEDICATION

J.A. Jubilee is the ultimate author of Heaven and Earth: The creator of life; a true redeemer, a rock in uncertain times, the essence of joy, and when faced with discomfort a comforter.

J.A. Jubilee knew us before he formed us in the womb: He knows the number of the very hairs on our heads; He knows our comings and our goings, and most important He knows our heart.

When I think about: the gift of life, present of free will, being cleansed of my sin, redeemed from death, and comforted in times of discomfort; I can truly celebrate with joy, acknowledge with thanksgiving, and be inspired to write for:

## JEHOVAH ALMIGHTY my JUBILEE

# Acknowledgments

When expressing my most profound level of gratitude and appreciation all glory, power, and praise belongs to Jehovah Almighty who is my: Creator, Redeemer, Comforter, and Joy. It is Him who has inspired me and allowed me to write the words contained in this book. I am truly blessed because of all the experiences I have encountered (good and bad) and count it all Joy. Also, for all the relationships he has given me, for each one is a genuine treasure far more priceless than any gem or material object on this Earth.

When reflecting on the many treasures, God has given me; my earthly parents are the epitome and iconic ambassadors of God who have given me a great start. My father, Deacon T.J. Faulk a well-respected Deacon and Teacher of the Bible who is not only meek, humble, and peaceful; he is a wonderful example of a disciple of God. As for my mother, Deaconess P. A. Faulk, she remains a loving disciplinarian and nurturer concerning decency and order.

To my loving wife, Carolyn who is a positive force in my life who consistently speaks life into everyone she meets. She is a beautiful example of a virtuous Proverb 31 woman who has endured many test, trials, and tribulations knowing that victory cannot and will not be taken from her.

To my son, T.J. Faulk III, a young man who engraves God's Laws in his heart and mind, and strives for excellence every day. I am so thankful God has allowed me to be a steward over your life. I can only hope and pray that God allows me to see you become the man he wants you to be, and father you have seen in me.

To my bonus children, Shanikqua, Kelvin, and Quinten, I am proud of each of you. You all have a beautiful soul that I know will be a blessing to anyone you encounter. May God continue to bless you with good health, peace, and joy.

To my loving and caring older sisters, LaCheryl, Teresa, and Marguerite; I am genuinely thankful for having such passionate siblings. Your over-protective love has cultivated my social skills, which has allowed me to increase my relationship treasures exponentially. I truly learned from all of you the application of Proverbs 18:24 - A man that hath friends must shew himself friendly.

**To the impactful Spiritual Leaders I have encountered:**

Pastor M. Robinson Jr. *** (First Baptist Church Wyandanch, NY)
Pastor C. Ridley *** (First Baptist Church Wyandanch, NY)
Pastor P. Bianco *** (Hollywood Baptist Church, Amityville, NY)
Pastor E. Meade (Church of God by Faith, Wyandanch, NY)
Pastor Dr. T. Everett (Bryant Swamp Missionary Baptist Church, Bladenboro, N.C.)
Bishop M. Talbert *** (First Church of Wyandanch, NY)
Pastor J. Branson (The Heart Church Ministries, Philadelphia, PA)
Pastor M. Chandler (Assembly of Prayer Baptist Church Roslyn, NY)
Pastor A. Stephens (Christian Service Foundation, Washington, D.C.)
Pastor Dr. C. Stanley (First Baptist Church of Atlanta, GA)
Pastor Dr. C. Oliver (Elizabeth Baptist Church, Atlanta GA)
Pastor V. Singletary (Round Branch Baptist Church, Bladenboro, N.C.)
Dr. J. Meyer (Joyce Meyer Ministries, St. Louis, Missouri)
Pastor Joel Osteen (Lakewood Church, Houston, TX)
Reverend K. Cochran (Elizabeth Baptist Church, Atlanta, GA)
Site Pastor T. Sims (Elizabeth Baptist Church, Douglasville, GA)
Minister T. Albritton (Elizabeth Baptist Church, Atlanta, GA)
Minister E. Towns (US House of Representatives NY $10^{th}$ District)
Minister M. Hadley (Elizabeth Baptist Church, Douglasville, GA)
Minister P. Phinisee (Elizabeth Baptist Church, Douglasville, GA)
Brother E. Keyton (Church of Christ at Bouldercrest Atlanta, GA)
Brother K. Teamer (Church of Christ at Bouldercrest, Atlanta, GA)
Brother O. Heyward (Church of Christ at West End, Atlanta, GA)
Pastor D. Hamilton (Winslow Baptist Church Sicklerville, NJ)
Minister N. & E. Ray (Linked Up Church, Powder Springs, GA)
Minister G. & C. Houston (Linked Up Church, Powder Springs, GA)

Note: *** Deceased

**Editorial and Review:**

C. McKnight
A. Davis
C. Faulk
T. J. Faulk III
M. Medlock
W. Graham
N. Turner
P. Phinisee
J. Ramsay
M. Gomes

**Photography – Book Cover:**

Keith Saunders – Marion Designs

Love and appreciation to my many friends I grew up with, work with, and fellowship with… You are all my true treasures on this earth, and the peace you give me is a consistent reminder that you being in my life is worth more than any materialistic item in the world.

Last but not least, my -eternal gratitude to all my readers.

Thank You.

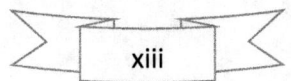

# **Prologue**

*The Israelites did evil in the eyes of the Lord; they forgot the Lord their God and served the Baals and the Asherahs*
*(Judges 3:7)*

*In those days there was no king in Israel, but every man did that which was right in his own eyes*
*(Judges 17:6)*

*No Mentors!*

*The Bible identifies forty-three (43) different Kings in the Old Testament that reigned over Israel and Judah.*

*Thirty-one (31) of them did Evil in the sight of the Lord.*

*Three (3) of them during their youth did right in the sight of the Lord but ended up doing evil by allowing the people to worship idols, images, and false gods.*
*(Solomon, Joash, and Amaziah)*

*One (1) of them was appointed, but not anointed as King.*
*(Ishbosheth – Saul's son)*

*One (1) of them was not stable, did good overall but followed the ways of Jeroboam in the end.*
*(Jehu)*

*However, seven (7) of them did right in the eyes of the Lord by putting away false gods and idols, but had setbacks in other areas of life.*

*(David, Asa, Jehoshaphat, Uzziah, Jotham, Hezekiah, and Josiah)*

*What was the one thing that separated the seven (7) Kings from the thirty-six (36) Kings?*

*They had Mentors!*

| Mentee | Mentor |
|---|---|
| David | Nathan and Gad (Prophet/Priest) |
| Asa | Azariah (Prophet) |
| Jehoshaphat | Asa (His father) |
| Uzziah/Azariah | Zechariah (Prophet) |
| Jotham | Uzziah/Azariah (His father) |
| Hezekiah | Isaiah (Prophet) |
| Josiah | Hilklah (Priest) |

Dear Reader,

I genuinely thank you for your support and interest. The book you are about to read is designed to spark conversation and thought with yourself and others. The style of writing is designed in a conversational format to maintain your interest. Each chapter articulates a specific purpose in mind; to address a person mentoring and a person receiving mentoring. In essence, it is as a Christian based guide to facilitate discussions for navigating life.

The Book has three (3) themes that expand over Twenty-two (22) chapters. To potentially expand on the reader's vocabulary (SAT/ACT Prep) I used words from one of my favorite self-enhancement books, *"1100 Words You Need to Know"*. Besides, I placed synonyms in parenthesis next to each word to maintain a good reading flow.

The Christian foundational teaching is an excellent start to help stimulate and create personal discussions when addressing life and its many choices. Also, foster an environment that reinforces one's Christian beliefs. Another dimension of this book is it allows you to self-reflect and build on your current knowledge. The last perspective is you can read simultaneously with a Mentor and Mentee to establish a core foundation and trust. This type of fellowship will galvanize discussions to branch off into additional topics and build on common interests.

As you embark on reading this book I can only hope you discover:

1. Reinforced knowledge of one's Christian faith
2. Introduce topics for mentoring discussions
3. Benefits of addressing life's issues with a positive attitude
4. Provide direction for career aspirations.

In essence, the primary goal of this book is to help you improve on your life's mission if you choose to accept it.

# Chapter 1 – Your Mission (Question)

*"Your Mission… if you choose to accept it?"* Is a question that derived from late 1960 to early 1970 TV show called *"Mission: Impossible."* An electronic recording device asked the initial question to a special agent confidentially and securely. If the special agent accepted the mission, he or she would continue to listen to the recording device. The recording would provide valuable (important) pieces of information:

1. Valuable intelligence information concerning opposition, enemy resistance, and environment;

2. Some rules, direction, and guidance to follow; and

3. The primary objective or goal of the mission.

After the information was explained, the agent was warned that the recording device would self-destruct in a certain amount of seconds. Unlike the recording device, this book "Will Not Self Destruct" after you read it. However, what remains is the question, "Your Mission… if you choose to accept it…?" is only a question you can answer.

At this time, you are probably wondering, "What is the Mission… so I can accept it or deny it?" Well to answer your question, it is a unique mission that few try to embark upon (take on). It requires you to be steadfast (loyal), immovable (can't be moved) and always abounding (plenty) in God's word as you serve as an agent/ambassador on this planet called earth. Now unlike the movies, you are not invited to be a secret or double agent/ambassador. O contraire, you are required to let your status and allegiance (stand for) be known to all you encounter (face) in support of recruitment activities, while you wear the full armor of God.

Your specific mission is simple; to serve God, then serve others. Although this seems to be too simple of an assignment, it can be complicated (difficult) by the things of this world and the fact that it is a commitment you take on for the rest of your life. The term commitment to some people is a sense of boredom or staleness. However, any commitment with God will never touch boredom and is the opposite of stale where you are constantly refreshed and renewed.

So, as you read each chapter of this book, reflect on how you a unique creation can:

1. Magnify (glorify) God

2. Serve others

3. Improving yourself

# Chapter 2 – Where Do I Start?

It's essential, *"If you desire anything in this world, and the world to come... a relationship with the living God is what your heart, soul, and flesh should cry out for...."* An excellent scripture that encapsulates (encloses) this is in Psalms 84:2:

> *"My soul longeth, yea, even fainteth for the courts of the Lord: my heart and my flesh crieth out for the living God." (KJV)*

Why may you ask? Well, God who is the creator of you and all the things around you is worthy and deserves the praise. He is your primary source of energy; just like a cell phone needs a charger, you should look to connect, pray, and fellowship with God to keep yourself charged. God, "The Great I Am" created you in His likeness for fellowship with you, a unique specimen who God breathed into for you to exist and "To be...."

WOW!!!! It's mind-blowing when the most Holy One and Creator of the Universe created you "To be...." That is a tall and wide order which seems like the sky is the limit. "To be" a level of "free will" that you can exercise with the Almighty's blessings… something you don't want to waste, abuse, or deny.

As for individuals who decide to be atheists (people who don't believe in God) and challenge God's existence. I would like to refer to what Albert Camus said, *"I would rather live my life as if there is a God and die to find out there isn't than live my life as if there isn't and die to find out there is...."* In essence, it's a Win-Win situation to serve Him. One thing is for sure; you are going to die. However, serving God during the life he has given you is your choice.  To be succinct (short), it's your mission… if you choose to accept it…?  I call it, "Mission Possible."

Now many people have gone to church at some point in their life.  If you left church feeling confused about the message you heard, the duration is too long or short, and some of the theatrics you may have experienced.  You are not alone.  I visited a church as a child where they did not have a children's church like they do these days; the type of church where a young person couldn't escape a long sermon he or she does not comprehend (understand), decipher (make clear) the songs sung, or prayers prayed.

Not to be facetious (funny), but I visited a church when I was five (5) years old.  I remember the pastor preaching as if he had asthma, finishing his sermon in a sweat.  The assisting pastor would drape the pastoral cloak over the preacher's back and walk him across the pulpit toward his chair.  The pastor would walk with a hunch back and dab the sweat from his brow.  Then all of a sudden he would get re-energized, throw the cloak onto the ground and come back to preach some more.  The church would roar with Amen and Hallelujah!

When I got older, I watched *"The Best of Eddie Murphy Saturday Night Live"* videotape.  I learned where this particular pastor mimicked this style… it was, James Brown!  In the video, Eddie was imitating James Brown getting into a hot tub and singing. To be honest, it was hysterically (uncontrolled emotion) funny.

Nonetheless, as I reflect on my own experiences in church, I'm thankful that my parents gave me an upbringing in a Bible teaching church.  At some point in my young adult life, I gained a better understanding of God and what He is all about.  It was that continuous exposure that gave me a good jump-start on life.  For that reason, I'm honestly a believer in Proverbs 22:6:

> *"Train up a child in the way he should go: and when he is old, he will not depart from it." (KJV)*

As a child, can I say that getting up early Sunday mornings to go to Sunday School and Church Service for a combined total of 5 hours was fun and fascinating (extremely interesting) Hmmmm…? Especially, when they expected a rambunctious (uncontrollable) little boy with vigor (energy) and curiosity (eager to know); to sit still and be quiet. "Yeah right…?"

In my teenage years, I learned which part of the service to sneak out of and when to sneak back in…. It was quite an operation, but my parents weren't unaware. Although my father said very little about it, my mother would remind me on occasion that I was not slick. Fortunately, she did not scold me too harshly. I guess they remembered what it was like to be a child sitting in church for what seemed to be an eternity. I would gather from their subtle and passive reaction that as long as I was in church hearing the message, songs, and prayers, it was good enough for them. Just the exposure alone would keep me close to what they were trying to instill in me, regardless of the breaks I took.

Church did have some characters, entertainers, and ego seekers. It was enough to deter anyone from wanting to show up, other than on Holidays like Easter and Christmas. Nevertheless, I recall one revival week when a preacher, Reverend Bianco who was genuine (real) about the events taking place in church delivered a serious message. The message stated that you must look beyond all of the negative aspects you see in church services as it is a diversion (change direction) created by the enemy. He challenged everyone to seek a personal relationship with God and not to worry about others. His summation was succinct (short) by just stating, *"Church is full of sinners; if sinners were not allowed in church, no one could be in attendance."*

The main thing that I extracted from his sermon was that I need to build a personal relationship with God. Regardless of the things I experienced in life, what other people were doing and how they were doing it…. I needed to build this relationship with God directly. No one else could do it for me.

With that understanding, my scrutiny (critical observation) of others started to diminish (decrease). I learned that I'm no better than anyone else, and no one is better than me…. I needed to stop worrying about how others worship the Lord and worship Him in my unique way;

because each human being is God's unique creation. A recent sermon I heard reminded me of this... John 21:20-22:

> *"Then Peter, turning about, seeth the disciple whom Jesus loved following; which also leaned on his breast at supper, and said, Lord which is he that betrayeth thee? Peter seeing him saith to Jesus, Lord, and what shall this man do? Jesus saith unto him, If I will that he tarry till I come, what is that to thee? Follow thou me." (KJV)*

In essence, try not to compare yourself to others, but focus on your relationship with God and love Him the way you know how to love.

Now how does one start to build a positive relationship with the Lord? Well, a good start is recognizing that God is an omnipotent (able to do anything) power who created the world and your life. Plus, realize that He sent His son to redeem (regain possession) humankind from the permanent sentence of death because of your sins and the sin brought in by Adam. Further, recognize the Holy Spirit as the comforter who comforts you in times of trials and tribulations.

Now does that mean you should be in complete isolation (alone)? The answer is no; you're encouraged to worship and fellowship with others. I'm quite sure there are a lot more good things that come out of church service than negative experiences; it depends on your mindset and what you choose to focus on, the negatives or the positives? Either way, count it all joy. Attending church and the gathering of the saints at any chance is viewed favorably by God. Doing this shows a high level of discipline (obey rules) and dedication (commitment). Plus, it is my belief and prayer that no matter what good or bad thing occurs in church service, each time you attend it edifies (builds) your spiritual growth and awareness. So seek every chance you get to be in a worship service that is for the Lord. If you feel uncomfortable in a church that is not teaching out of the Bible with too much theatrics (dramatic performances) find another church that caters (feeds) to your spiritual needs.

In the past, I relocated to another State, and I went out looking for a church to join. I came across this urban style church with a gothic (middle ages) appeal. The preacher went on about his political views and opinions with only vague (unclear) references to the Bible. He even mentioned that if you wanted to hear more about the Bible, attend Bible Study. That alone told me this is "NOT" the church for me. I like to attend services where I'm learning and experiencing information that has a biblical basis. Therefore, if the word of God is absent from a particular church, you should be as well.

Several years back I went to the movies with an associate who enjoyed horror movies, while I enjoyed comedy. So we compromised and watched Eddie Murphy's movie, *Vampire in Brooklyn*. There was a scene in which a corrupt (dishonest) visiting preacher's body was possessed by the Vampire's spirit, both roles played by Eddie Murphy. After being possessed by the spirit, the preacher was unable to go into the church. So he cajoled (convinced) the congregation to stand outside where he delivered his sermon on, *"Evil being Good."* At the end of his sermon he had the mindless congregation singing, *"Evil is Good."* Now that started a revolution (complete change) in my mind that forced me to ask myself, whether I was making myself knowledgeable of God's words? Was I allowing myself to fall victim to false teaching that may not be of God? After all, the enemy is bold enough and knowledgeable in the Bible to walk into any pulpit and deliver a sermon to convict (make guilty) the masses. This revolutionary thought galvanized (bring about action) a drive within me to make sure I understood God's word and to strengthen my spiritual being with the ability to identify any possible false teachings. I looked in my Bible and Bible Dictionary to identify the authors of a book, when they possibly wrote it, and who the message was intended for....

Indeed the Bible is written by man, which many would contend that man is fallible (in error); therefore the Bible is fallible. However, the Bible was written by men who were "inspired" by God through the Holy Spirit; who purified (made clean) the words men wrote, therefore, making the Bible a perfect instrument from God.

*"Thy word is a lamp unto my feet and a light unto my path" (Psalms 119:105 KJV)*

When you commit (become loyal) to God by believing in His Son's salvation (delivered from harm) and grace (divine assistance); then submit to His will. Seek what He stands for and what He does not stand for…. In life, before you join any club, association, or group, you should at least know something about the rules and what is expected of you and its members.

When it comes to God's associations, seek the salvation provided (given) by Christ and the laws created by God. When I attended church growing up, I cannot recall hearing a preacher preach about the Ten Commandments (Even with some of the churches having the Commandments framed in a corner). I listened to all types of sermons, but no one in my past has ever stopped to break down the Ten Commandments and how viable (important) they are in maintaining a relationship with God, especially after you recognize Christ as your deliverer (rescuer).

An excellent start is to engrave (cut a design into) His Ten Commandments into your heart and mind. To make sure every thought, action, or reaction is not in breach (breaking) of the laws given by God.

Many know, man alone has millions of laws concerning plenty of issues that are: codified (changed), rescinded (taken back), debated (argued), and hated. However, God has Ten Commandments with additional commandments given by His Son that ties them all together. The funny part about this is that we have the nerve to call God complex and a mystery when it is man who is the mystery. We can't keep our laws in order, but God's laws remain unchanged. The truth is: God is trustworthy and straightforward.

His son Jesus supports God's Law in Matthew 5:17:

*"Think not that I am come to destroy the law, or the prophets: I am not come to destroy, but to fulfill." (KJV)*

To recap this chapter, the steps toward doing the right thing are simple:

1. Make a commitment in your heart; decide in your mind that you want a personal relationship with God and that believing

in the salvation and grace provided by His son is the perfect place to start.

2. Make it a habit of speaking to God every day.

3. Start by reading your Bible, "A chapter a day keeps the enemy at bay."

A quote made by Malcolm X: *"If you don't stand for something… you'll fall for anything…"* When it comes to God, "If you don't stand for God's Commandments… you will fall for anything and everything else; along with the rest of this fallen world."
To strengthen this point in Hosea 4:6:

*"My people for lack of knowledge: because thou hast rejected knowledge, I will also reject thee, that thou shalt be no priest to me: seeing thou hast forgotten the law of thy God, I will also forget your children." (KJV)*

During your time on earth, do not let God forget you or your children by ignoring his law.

To add what Christ's says in Mark 7:6-9:

*"This people honoureth me with their lips, but their heart is far from me. Howbeit in vain do they worship me, teaching for doctrines the commandments of men. For laying aside the commandment of God, ye hold the tradition of men, as the washing of pots and cups: and many other such like things ye do. And he said unto them, Full well ye reject the commandment of God, that ye may keep your own tradition." (KJV)*

# Chapter 3 – Rules of Engagement

The Ten Commandments are the ground rules from the Old Testament that are in no way canceled out, but Christ came to fulfill them as expressed in Matthew 5:17. In essence, Christ came to show us how to live by the Commandments being that all of humankind remains unable to fulfill the Law through our inherited fallen/sinful nature.

**Ten Commandments:**

***COMMANDMENT ONE: THOU SHALT HAVE NO OTHER GODS BEFORE ME*** *(Exodus 20:3 KJV)*

Justification: God is a Jealous God, to put any other God or thing that does not exist above Him and His power is an insult. To avoid breaking this commandment: try not to look to different ideologies (mythology), Ba'als (false gods), worshipping materialistic items, the praise of one's self, or race. No one or thing has done for you what God has done for you. He supplies all your needs and wants.

Empathy: Looking at it from God's perspective (view), say you purchased a gift for a dear friend, how would you feel if the friend who received the gift turned around and gave credit to someone else for buying the gift? I guarantee you would be infuriated (angry), I know I would be…. So, can you blame God for creating this commandment, and for keeping it simple?

**COMMANDMENT TWO: THOU SHALT NOT MAKE UNTO THEE ANY GRAVEN IMAGE, OR ANY LIKENESS OF ANYTHING THAT IS IN HEAVEN ABOVE, OR THAT IS IN THE EARTH BENEATH, OR THAT IS IN THE WATER UNDER THE EARTH; AND NOT BOW DOWN THYSELF TO THEM, NOR SERVE THEM...** *(Exodus 20:4-5 KJV)*

Justification: This kind of ties in with the first commandment, but expands a little further. God is a jealous God, do not make something and bow down to worship it, even if you think it is a symbol of the Almighty Himself. In essence, God is greater than any image or thing made by man (house, car, jewelry, furniture, apparel, statue, etc...). Further, for man to create, then encapsulate (confine) an image of God in a non-living object is an insult to God and the true order of creation. The order being, God created man then gave him dominion (authority) over all the earth and animals.

Empathy: God is so great, omnipotent (all powerful) and ubiquitous (everywhere, omnipresent) it is an insult to compress all that power and authority into an image made by man. Further, God is a God of the living and to contain His existence into things that are not living through an object is a contradiction (contrary) of who God is.

**COMMANDMENT THREE: THOU SHALT NOT TAKE THE NAME OF THE LORD THY GOD IN VAIN** *(Exodus 20:7 KJV)*

Justification: When reviewing the third commandment, you are drawn to the word *vain*. The word has several meanings that point in one direction; negative connotations (meaning). In the context of the Bible *in vain* means: to no avail, misrepresentation, without success, in a disrespectful manner (cursing). God is all about action and success. To use the Lord's name in vain is not being truthful to God's power as the creator of all things. So by cursing with His name or expressing "God Said..." without Him saying it... is a sin within itself (see commandment nine). A more concise (short) example of this commandment is the idea of proclaiming (announcing) you are God's child, but consistently are (publically or privately) in violation of His commandments… that is truly taking the name of the Lord in vain.

Empathy: One cannot profess (claim) to know God if he/she is violating any of the outlined commandments, or questions His existence. Another perspective is when looking at the creation of the world God spoke everything he thought into existence. Being that He created us in His likeness; we too can speak things into existence. However, the difference between God and man are the factors of dimensions and time, meaning God can speak and the change is instantaneously (right away). When we speak, it can happen, but within a certain season. That is why you have to be careful of what you say. A superb scripture is in Proverbs 18:21: *Death and life is in the power of the tongue…*. Even idle talk is looked down upon because it goes nowhere, and as expressed earlier, God is a God of action which nothing He does is in vain. Therefore, do not speak something that does not represent God, or contradicts your allegiance to Him.

## COMMANDMENT FOUR: REMEMBER THE SABBATH DAY, TO KEEP IT HOLY *(Exodus 20:8 KJV)*

Justification: Indeed the Sabbath day is a day of rest because it is a day the Lord hath made for rest. God rested from all His creations; then He blessed the day and hallowed it (holy). Over time, man has taken this commandment completely to the extreme, but Jesus came to set the record straight (Matthew 12:10-12):

> *"And, behold, there was a man which had his hand withered. And they asked him (Jesus), saying, Is it lawful to heal on the Sabbath days? That they might accuse him. And he said unto them, What man shall there be among you, that shall have one sheep, and if it fall into a pit on the Sabbath day, will he not lay hold on it, and lift it out? How much then is a man better than a sheep? Wherefore it is lawful to do well on the Sabbath days."*

Therefore, trying to gain an advantage on this day is a taboo.

Empathy: Yes, the Sabbath is holy, so do your best to take it easy and reflect on the week that past, just like God did when He reflected on all

His creations. Besides, Christ explained that you should *"do well…"* but in no way is it limited to just the Sabbath. Here is another little tidbit of information - the Sabbath is on Saturday. There were lots of debates on what day the Sabbath falls on, but the answer is Saturday. Most Christians rest and worship on Sunday, the main reason for that is because Jesus Christ rose on a Sunday Morning, which is the first day of the week. Therefore, most Christians have changed the day of worship from Saturday to Sunday.

## COMMANDMENT FIVE: HONOUR THY FATHER AND THY MOTHER *(Exodus 20:12 KJV)*

Justification: Another key word that jumps out at you is *honor* which means: *"highest respect, as for special merit, esteem"* (Webster's Dictionary). The respect and esteem you give must be directed at those who birthed you, if your natural parents are not around, to those who have taken care of you and probably still take care of you. Keep in mind that you honor your parents even when they are not in your presence; your appearance (clothes and hygiene), speech, and interactions should express and imply that your parents raised you right as a form of Honor. If you are unable to respect the people who provide for you and love you, how can you respect God who provides all things and you cannot even see Him?

Expansion: According to the rest of Exodus 20:12:

> *"that their days on the earth may be long upon the land which the Lord thy God giveth thee" (KJV).*

In other words: by not respecting your parents, you are an accident looking for a place to happen. You are in some form or fashion shortening your time possessing the gifts God has given (your time on this earth).

Yes, there are parents out there that do things to their children that damage them in so many ways (mentally, socially, financially, and physically). However, that is never a cause or reason for this commandment to be broken. If damaged or harmed by a parent, you should articulate your pain. However, if your parents do not wish to hear from you, your silence in their presence should serve as a reminder of the pain you are experiencing. In no way should you verbally disparage them to their face or behind their back. Your silence enough serves as a form of honor, especially when in pain. We are all accountable to God; for a parent, any wrong committed toward children, God will hold that parent accountable. At some point in time children grow up and become parents and will probably make a mistake or two, but it is no cause for a child to dishonor their parent and to break the order of honor set by God through this commandment. Just remember, it is God who will elevate you out of any harmful situation, and it starts with obeying "all" of His commandments.

### COMMANDMENT SIX: THOU SHALT NOT KILL *(Exodus 20:13 KJV)*

Justification: There are some arguments and further explanations that may be required. To kill an animal for its meat is acceptable: to kill it unnecessarily is not acceptable. To kill another human being serves no purpose at all. To deprive a man of his free will on this earth is wrong and to take a life without cause is wrong. What may be exempt from this is war and capital punishment, which falls on a government's leadership. On an individual basis, self-defense is acceptable.

Expansion: Look to accomplish good rather than evil, look to forgive rather than not forgive, and look to extend mercy before seeking justice. When it is all said and done a great deal of us are violators of the laws and rules established by God. Yet, through His Son's sacrifice and grace, we have a second chance. So why not extend forgiveness to your brethren as a reminder of God's mercy and favor over your life.

Martin Luther King Jr: *"If we do an eye for an eye and a tooth for a tooth, we will be a blind and toothless nation."*

## COMMANDMENT SEVEN: THOU SHALT NOT COMMIT ADULTERY *(Exodus 20:14 KJV)*

Justification: When looking at adultery, it is the act of breaking an agreement. The most commonly known agreement is that of marriage. It is a contract between a male and a female, with vows taken before God that are clear and easy to remember, even by those who are not married. *"Forsake all others… until death do you part…."* God outlined this when He gave it to Moses in Genesis 2:24: *"Therefore shall a man leave his Father and Mother, and shall cleave unto his wife: and they shall be one flesh."*

Expansion: God admires good contracts with Him and amongst one another. To break an agreement that we take before the Lord is a breach of contract, which is similar to breaking decency and order. God is all about decency and order. In essence, your word is your bond. As for fornication, it is the willingness to partake in the consummation (complete) process without a contract. That alone is out of order with what God intended. The protocol (procedure) is simple: make your vows of commitment, then consummate. When it comes to marriage, the act of reproductive organ consummation serves as a blood covenant between a man and a woman, where the woman (supposedly a virgin) bleeds upon initial intercourse and the two become one flesh. Also, God set a mandate for man and woman to reproduce into the earth which can only be done by reproductive organs/members. As for couples trying to multiply and replenish the earth with no success, their connecting by their reproductive organs makes them one flesh and remains honorable before God (Barren women of the Bible who later conceived by God's authority: Sarah, Rebekah, Rachel, Manoah, Hannah, and Elizabeth). Genesis 1:27-28

> *"So God created man in his image, in the image of God created he him; male and female created he them. And God blessed them, and God said unto them, Be fruitful, and multiply, and replenish the earth, and subdue it: and have*

*dominion over the fish of the sea, and over the fowl of the air, and over every living thing that moveth upon the earth".*

In the Old Testament days, God made covenants with Israel that were consistently broken, making them an adulterous nation. The process of getting back into agreement with God required sacrifices of animals that served as the consummation of an agreement between God and man, & man and man. With the New Testament, blood sacrifices are no longer required because Jesus Christ served as the pure sacrifice and lamb, for the remission of all of our sins. The main point is to enter into good agreements that are anointed by God and consummate them properly (handshake, signing a document, or reproductive organ consummation for marriages). To breach an agreement, not enter into a contract when it is required, or entering into a bad agreement is not of God and His order.

### COMMANDMENT EIGHT: THOU SHALT NOT STEAL
*(Exodus 20:15 KJV)*

Justification: To take without permission while depriving our fellow brethren of something you did not earn through fair and an equitable agreement. Also, taking something in the absence of a contract/agreement (verbal or written), or knowledgeable, fair trade (cheating, misleading) is not of God or His order.

Expansion: The act of taking assets, relationships, land, and ideas without permission deprives our fellow brethren of what is rightfully theirs. In essence, being the cause of someone's loss can only plant and harbor ill feelings with resentment.

### COMMANDMENT NINE: THOU SHALT NOT BEAR FALSE WITNESS AGAINST THY NEIGHBOUR *(Exodus 20:16 KJV)*

Justification: Misrepresenting (falsifying) information about anyone or thing; exaggerations and understatements also fall under this category. To lie is the complete opposite of God, "truth." Even the idea of believing an unconfirmed rumor could put you in jeopardy of violating this commandment because your mind is holding a possible false truth.

Expansion: Any person would get upset if someone misrepresented information about them. Hence anyone could empathize with a victim of a mendacious (false) tale. Further, to carry gossip without confirming facts, one can be indirectly guilty of violating this commandment for carrying false truths. That is why it is essential to stay away from gossip and gossipers. Their negative mentality is contagious (spread) and could inadvertently (mistake) pull you away from what God stands for, *truth*. Also, the idea of casting judgment based on superficial (shallow) facts or prejudice without seeking all the facts and ignoring facts is the sin of presumption (opinion).

## *COMMANDMENT TEN: THOU SHALT NOT COVET THY NEIGHBOUR'S HOUSE* (Exodus 20:17 KJV)

Justification: The desiring of another person's: assets, relationship, position (career), or property.

Expansion: God has created each of us as unique beings and has apportioned us with what He sees fit. Therefore, everyone should be content with what God has given them stewardship over without desiring their neighbor's lot/possessions/relationships. Focusing on what our neighbor has leads to envy, which pulls you away from God and the purpose He has for your life. Focusing on others status, relationships and materialistic things pull our energy away to a point where we forget the things that are important to God. Keep in mind, your most prized possessions in life are your family and friends, not material things you acquire and can't love you back.

# JESUS ADDS TWO MORE COMMANDMENTS (Mark 12 30&31)

***JESUS COMMANDMENT: THOU SHALT LOVE THE LORD THY GOD WITH ALL THY HEART, AND ALL THY SOUL, AND WITH ALL THY MIND*** *(Matthew 22:37 & Mark 12:30 KJV)*

Justification: If you love God with all your heart, soul, and mind. You are aware and embrace that God is the source of everything that exists and you respect Him and all His creations. If you love God with all your heart, you would not have to be concerned with breaking any of the commandments mentioned in this chapter.

Empathy: A comparison of this commandment with some of the older: If you are loving God you will not have any other Gods. If you are loving God, you won't have any graven images and serving them. If you are loving God, you won't take His name in vain. If you are loving God, you will remember to keep the Sabbath Holy. And If you are loving God, you will honor your Mother and Father.

***JESUS COMMANDMENT: THOU SHALT LOVE THY NEIGHBOUR AS THYSELF*** *(Matthew 22:39 & Mark 12:31 KJV)*

Justification: If you love your neighbor as yourself, you are being put into your neighbor shoes to bring about a degree of empathy (being able to relate). Therefore, allowing you to understand your neighbor's position if they become a victim.

Expansion: A comparison of this commandment with some of the older: If you love your neighbors as thyself, you don't want to harm them. If you love your neighbors, you won't think about taking part in breaking up their marriage or relationships. If you love your neighbors, you won't think about stealing from them. If you love your neighbors, you won't think about telling false tales about them. And if you love your neighbors, you will appreciate their uniqueness and respect the lot God has entrusted to them for stewardship.

The two additional Commandments given by Christ (Mark 12:30&31 KJV) are "Reemphasized Commandments" that are in essence a quicker curtailed version of all the original commandments. Once again, Christ came not to destroy the law but to fulfill the commandments. The Commandments exist today and tomorrow, but it is through the sacrifice of Christ that we can obtain forgiveness for violating the commandments when we repent entirely.

To recap this chapter, the steps toward doing the right thing are simple:

1. Start by engraving (carving) God's Ten Commandments in your heart and mind. Know them, be them, live them.

2. Recite (speak) them before starting your day, and compare your successes and failures at the end of each day.

3. Any failures, repent; if you offend someone plan to apologize immediately.

4. No man or woman born of Adam could fulfill the Commandments.

5. Jesus magnified the Ten Commandments through His living and simplified them through the two commandments He gave.

In Ecclesiastes Chapter 12 verse 13 to 14:

*"Now all has been heard; here is the conclusion of the matter: Fear God and keep his commandments, for this is the duty of all mankind. For God will bring every deed into judgment, including every hidden thing, whether it is good or evil." (KJV)*

Romans Chapter 13 verse 9:

*"For this, Thou shalt not commit adultery, Thou shalt not kill, Thou shalt not steal, Thou shalt not bear false witness, Thou shalt not covet; and if there be any other commandment, it is briefly comprehended in this saying, namely, Thou shalt love thy neighbour as thyself." (KJV)*

| Question: Jesus Additional Commandment One (God First): | Answer: | Ten Commandments: |
|---|---|---|
| If you are… loving God with all your heart, soul, mind, and strength? | You are not… | having other Gods |
| If you are… loving God with all your heart, soul, mind, and strength? | You are not… | making graven images, or bowing to worship them |
| If you are… loving God with all your heart, soul, mind, and strength? | You are not… | taking the name of the Lord in vain |
| If you are… loving God with all your heart, soul, mind, and strength? | You are not… | forgetting the Sabbath and keeping it un-holy |
| If you are… loving God with all your heart, soul, mind, and strength? | You are not… | dishonoring your Mother and Father |
| If you are… loving God with all your heart, soul, mind, and strength? | You are not… | killing |
| If you are… loving God with all your heart, soul, mind, and strength? | You are not… | comitting adultery |
| If you are… loving God with all your heart, soul, mind, and strength? | You are not… | stealing |
| If you are… loving God with all your heart, soul, mind, and strength? | You are not… | bearing false witness |
| If you are… loving God with all your heart, soul, mind, and strength? | You are not… | coveting your neighbor's house |
| Question: Jesus Additional Commandment Two (People Second): | Answer: | Ten Commandments: |
| If you are… loving your neighbor as yourself? | You are not… | dishonoring your Mother and Father (Authoratative neighbors) |
| If you are… loving your neighbor as yourself? | You are not… | killing your neighbors |
| If you are… loving your neighbor as yourself? | You are not… | comitting adultery with and against your neighbor |
| If you are… loving your neighbor as yourself? | You are not… | stealing from your neighbor |
| If you are… loving your neighbor as yourself? | You are not… | bearing false witness against your neighbor |
| If you are… loving your neighbor as yourself? | You are not… | coveting your neighbor's house |

# Chapter 4 – Things God Despises
(Sins of the Heart and Soul)

It is clear that the Ten Commandments represents how we should respect God and interact with others, but how do we deal with our internal conflicts? Within each of us, there are deep internal battles that we must wrestle and defeat to truly master ourselves. The essence of these internal battles requires us to have a certain mindset, control our thoughts, and minimize (reduce) or eliminate (remove) negative actions and reactions.

To present some biblical history, in the beginning when Adam ate of the forbidden fruit (after Eve) both their eyes were opened. By eating of the forbidden fruit, both knew of good and evil (Genesis 3:6, 7, and 22). With that being the case, the internal conflict within each man is passed down through Adam's sin, which explains the reason for our internal and external battles.

To reiterate from Chapter 3, know the Commandments by heart. Yet, the real challenge is living by them and under the salvation given by Christ. God's laws allow you to be in direct and clear communication with Him and receipt of His many blessings.

For example, many computer or communication technicians are familiar with system protocols (rules) that are required for two or more devices to communicate with one another (Phone or Computer). If one step of the protocol is missing, the communication fails, or the transmission between the systems is distorted (unclear).

When reviewing the Creator's commandments, one should view them as system protocols to follow to have clear communication with God and for Him to find favor and rest in you. As many know, God will <u>not</u> dwell where things are in violation, or out of order (Once again, there's that word, *order*). To expand on this, God hears the prayers of those who are loyal to His commandments, have innocent hearts, and repented (sorry) sinners who are humble. One Bible scripture that covers Christ's view on the topic is found in Luke 18:10-14:

> *"Two men went up into the temple to pray: the one a Pharisee, and the other a publican. The Pharisee stood and prayed thus with himself, God, I thank thee, that I am not as other men are, extortioners, unjust, adulterers, or even as this publican. I fast twice a week, I give tithes of all that I possess. And the publican standing afar off, would not lift up so much as his eyes unto heaven, but smote upon his breast, saying, God be merciful to me a sinner. I tell you, this man went down to his house justified rather than the other: for every one that exalteth himself shall be abased; and he that humbleth himself shall be exalted."(KJV)*

To help us understand our internal battles, God inspired Solomon the wisest and richest King of all the earth, to explain how God sees things by writing the book of Proverbs and other books of the Bible. A great way to allow the Lord to find rest in you is by mastering your internal battles and being conscious of the thoughts and acts He despises, which is in Proverbs 6:16-20:

> *"These six things doth the Lord hate: yea, seven are an abomination unto him:*
>
> 1. *A proud look*
> 2. *A lying tongue*
> 3. *Hands that shed innocent blood*
> 4. *A heart that deviseth wicked imaginations*
> 5. *Feet that be swift in running to mischief*
> 6. *A false witness that speaketh lies*
> 7. *He that soweth discord among brothers*
>
> *My son, keep thy father's commandment, and forsake not the law of thy mother." (KJV)*

To consider holding any of these behavioral traits means you are further away from God than you want to be. The next few pages address the things God despises and how they match to specific commandments He gave man.

First, *a proud look* gives an indication (sign) that a person has excessive (too much) belief in one's self, which leaves little to no room for God. Now it is perfectly fine to have confidence in oneself, but to be excessive is where the sin rests (a thin line between arrogance and confidence). When reviewing the commandments, pride violates the first commandment. *Thou shalt have no other God before him* (including yourself). The conduct that opposes pride is humility, which means to humble yourself when you accomplish good things. According to Proverbs 27:1:

*"Boast not thyself of to-morrow; for thou knowest not what a day may bring forth." (KJV)*

Plus, don't seem bothered when someone is tooting their own horn or of others, because their boasting (brag) is their sin before God. Nonetheless, look to be appreciative (thankful) of others and their accomplishments.

Second, *a lying tongue* does not represent the truth and can create disorder. A lying tongue violates the ninth commandment of bearing false witness against thy neighbor. When you choose in your mind to bear false witness, you are choosing to be the opposite of what God stands for, Truth. To counter bearing false witness, it is easier and shorter, to tell the truth than a lie. To say one lie often leads to another and another, which is mentally exhausting. Besides, it can lead to the third concern outlined by Solomon.

Third, *shedding of innocent blood* can be directly or indirectly related to bearing false witness. Or, knowing the truth and not saying anything to exonerate (free) someone who may be falsely accused (WOW!). Indeed, you may not say anything that is false. However, to say nothing about something you know when an innocent life is on the line can cause you to violate other laws like the sixth commandment of *thou shalt not kill*. To be honest, you are guilty by association.

Fourth, *a heart that deviseth wicked imaginations* lead to breaking three or more commandments (killing, adultery, and stealing), even if it is a latent reactionary thought to someone who has wronged you. It could lead to bearing false witness and coveting what your neighbor possesses either materialistic (greedy) things or social status. To sit around and devise wicked things distorts your being, along with your communication and association with God.

Fifth, *feet that be swift in running to mischief,* goes hand and hand with the fourth one *heart that deviseth wicked imaginations* in regards to the commandments that are breached (broken). It even takes it one step further because you are no longer thinking, but acting on thoughts as an advocate (representative) of mischievous (naughty) things. Once again, this is contrary (opposite) to what God stands for….

Sixth, *a false witness that speaketh lies* directly refers to bearing false witness. To claim knowledge concerning an event, you never witnessed is a false witness. To bear false witness means you are not an advocate of the truth and in no way could commune with God who stands for truth yesterday, today, and tomorrow. As pointed out earlier, even to keep a silent tongue while someone is falsely accused makes you a bearer of false truths by association. In other words, if you are fearful of telling the truth, you are letting fear control you.

Last, *soweth discord among brethren,* can be in breach of multiple commandments which you become an advocate (supporter) for war and not peace. In essence, try not to be the bearer of gossip. Let idle (inactive) talk remain as idle talk. If someone should confide in you with their opinions don't be the little bird that conveys a person's thoughts, they may lead to actions that violate God's commandments. Plus, do not create fabrications (false) to bring about a conflict for the value of entertainment.

I recall in elementary school; there was a young boy who liked to see people fight because that was what his entire family enjoyed. So he would go to one boy and say, "Such and such was talking bad about your mother and you." The receiver of such information would get his dander up and respond with insults about the unsuspecting contender of this plot. Then the contender would get wind of what was said and respond in kind until the two met to settle this matter with their fist. The sad part was that neither one of them ever confirmed whether the negative comments were ever even said. Each person's first reaction was to get upset, which baited (trapped) them in for a conflict in which reputations (pride) had to be protected. With that being the ingredients, hostilities were set in motion even after the physical altercation, no matter who won or lost. In God's eyes, all lost; it was a lose-lose situation. The only way to avoid this is to remain peaceful, confirm and confront all rumors (hearsay), or ignore them in its entirety. Respect people's opinions, negative or positive, and don't get consumed by mischief. If someone was to bring a rumor to you, your response should be, "Is that right… well if that is so, I'm not offended." (Don't forget to smile and walk away). It is a statement of neutrality (taking no side). Never react in anger as it takes up too much energy. However, immediately consult with any source of an alleged comment to dispel (dismiss) all negative perceptions or false statements and to set any record straight. To not address certain rumors or mendacious (false) tales at the source can be an inadvertent (unintended) admission.

In this life, people are going to say what they want and feel. What matters is God's view of you. In the Bible, the Books of Judges, Kings, and Samuel you'll read about many Judges and Kings. It summarizes their overall life grade based on their actions from the perspective of the Lord, "*Did good or evil in the sight of the Lord.*" My goal on judgment day is to hear my name and that I did well in the sight of the Lord… to be succinct (brief) that is all that matters.

Another list of taboos to be aware of is not directly in the Bible but is a relevant topic, *"The Seven Deadly Sins"* which in a way co-insides with the book called Dante's Inferno. *(www.deadlysins.com)*:

1. Pride
2. Envy
3. Gluttony
4. Lust
5. Anger
6. Greed
7. Sloth

Once again, *pride is excessive confidence in one's self, which is something that takes you away from God.* To compare yourself to others is leading you down the path of pride. Even comparing your own: heritage, race, ethnicity, or religion is a form of pride that is unacceptable. Therefore to repeat, combat this with humility (humble). Learn to appreciate others' experiences and what they have to offer. Humble yourself and be willing to hear of others success and learn from them.

*"Pride is the idolatrous worship of ourselves, and that is the national religion of hell." Alan Redpath*

*Envy is the desire of traits, status, abilities, or situation of others.* To be jealous or dogmatic about someone's *lot* (possessions or characteristics) goes hand and hand with pride as well. To want what others have and despise or discriminate (separate) based on that is envy. To counter this, practice love and put peace in your heart when meeting and dealing with people. Look for the good in others and eliminate speaking ill of others at the same time.

*"A sound heart is the life of the flesh: but envy the rottenness of the bones." (Proverb 14:30 KJV)*

*Gluttony is the desire to consume more than what is required*; this applies to food, entertainment, alcohol, and other goods. Too much of a good thing can consume you. For example, playing video games constantly or overeating can bring about adverse effects. To fight this, practice temperance, which is to accept natural limits and restrain yourself when the temptation to take more is present. For example, certain celebrations or holidays are a prime time to over-indulge. To help you in this battle, before any event or situation that brings about the opportunity to consume excessively (alcohol or food), make a plan ahead on what your level of consumption (taking in) will be and stick to it. When you become the legal age, and you're going to attend a social gathering where drinking will be involved, make it a plan to consume no drinks, or no more than two drinks the entire evening. Personally, the consumption of alcohol is not a taboo. However, to drink excessively is where the sin resides. Keep in mind, Noah made a vineyard, and Jesus turned water into wine.

*Lust is the craving pleasures for your body.* There are several opinions on what constitutes lust. A good viewpoint is that it is not a sin to notice a good-looking person; however, to stare and undress them in your mind is crossing the line into lust. To undress them in your mind means to imagine what they look like without clothes. Further, lust does not apply to just sexual desires it applies to material things as well (sports car, jewelry, clothes, etc…).

*Anger is in the heart of individuals who are ready to strike instead of embracing love.* It is a desire to strive for wrath. For the most part, anger is part of a reaction to an action or a mistake made by someone else (even one's self). It is a choice, which we seldom (rare) practice to control. To combat anger, exercise kindness when something adverse (hostile) occurs. Do yourself a favor by planning what you may say or do if an accident happens, like a car accident, or when someone breaks a most prized possession of yours. Keep in mind that human emotions and feelings are more fragile (easily broken) and vulnerable (weak) and cannot be restored, as for material possessions things can be replaced. Just convince yourself that if something is damaged or someone offends you, it will cost you nothing to keep a cool head and maintain favor with God. If an object was broken or something said to hurt your feelings, *it is what it is*. Words and materialistic (worldly) objects are what they are here today, gone tomorrow. You can't take them with you when you die. However, it is the good memories that you leave with your family and friends that are more valuable. If an item breaks, it was meant to be broken; maybe you were favoring it too much. If something was said, perhaps it was said to test your reaction and to see if you are practicing kindness instead of wrath. Lord knows you would want kind treatment if you broke something or said something unintentionally (accident) that was offensive. All of life is a test and full of choices, if you commit in your heart and mind to choose kindness each time, it will soon turn into a habit that defines your character.

*Greed is the desire for material wealth or gain, which causes you to ignore the spiritual realm.* Greed thrives (increases) on getting one's fair share and more. To combat this, practice generosity (kind) which means giving without expecting anything in return. The practice alone can help this fallen world to be a better place. Just keep in mind, when there is greed, there is poverty. If people were more spiritual and generous, poverty could be eliminated.

Last, *sloth is the avoidance of spiritual and physical work.* I have seen companies collapse because of slothful (lazy) high-level executives who would instead tell tales of a company's earnings than to figure out how to earn money for a company. To fight this, be an enthusiastic (eager) person who is ready to respond to work and God's commandments. Exercise the energy God has given you which is the reason why you're here. To produce into the earth is what man is called to do. Even Adam (before given a wife) had a task assigned by God (cultivating and naming the animals). So it is a part of God's order for you to work and not lay around on the backs of others.

The book of Proverbs Chapter 6 and the seven deadly sins were identified to help give some guidance and understanding of what God despises. Yes, life is tough, but it is more tolerable if you can instill in your mind the things God likes and flee from the things He despises. In essence, try to turn your thoughts and actions into habits that are worthy of God's fellowship and many blessings.

There is one other thing that is highly important and considered unforgivable as outlined by Christ in Matthew Chapter 12:31-32:

> *"Wherefore I say unto you, All manner of sin and blasphemy shall be forgiven unto men: but the blasphemy against the Holy Spirit shall not be forgiven unto men. And whosoever speaketh a word against the Son of man, it shall be forgiven him: but whosoever speaketh against the Holy Ghost, it shall not be forgiven him, neither in this world, neither in the world to come." (KJV)*

According to Nelson's Bible Dictionary, *blasphemy is the act of cursing, slandering, reviling, showing contempt, or lack of reverence.* In essence, to commit blasphemy against the Holy Spirit is to take the work of the Holy Spirit, and claim it was Satan's work (some of the Jews did this during the time Christ was on Earth).

To recap this chapter of the book:

1. Know the things God despises and avoid them.

2. Be knowledgeable of the seven deadly sins.

3. Briefly, anticipate offenses and things that bother you. Have a prepared mental plan concerning your reaction that is favorable in the sight of God. (Run brief mental scenarios in your mind). Be prepared to expect good things, but mindful of the unexpected.

4. Never commit blasphemy against the Holy Spirit, remain silent or reserved when witnessing miracles or events. Give the comforter credit for all good things and concerning questionable things remain silent.

A person who takes that closer walk with God is on a journey that can lead to isolation (loneliness), but they are respected, and people will confide in them. Their silence/humble nature alone makes them favored among God; and wise to a person in trouble. By avoiding these sins and embracing the virtues (good qualities) that combat them allows you to preserve the real treasures of this earth, your family and friends.

A good set of scriptures to read that expands even more on what God despises is found in Romans 1:28 to 32:

*"And even as they did not like to retain God in their knowledge, God gave them over to a reprobate mind, to do those things which are not convenient; being filled with all unrighteousness, fornication, wickedness, covetousness, maliciousness, full of envy, murder, debate, deceit, malignity, whispers, backbiters, haters of God, despiteful, proud, boasters, inventors of evil things, disobedient to parents, without understanding, covenant-breakers, without natural affection, implacable, unmerciful: who knowing the judgment of God,*

*that they which commit such things are worthy of death, not only do the same, but have pleasure in them that do them." (KJV)*

Before ending this chapter concerning our internal conflicts, it is important to highlight what Christ expressed in his Sermon on the Mount that starts in Matthew Chapter 5. The entire topic emphasizes the mindset we must have to gain God's divine favor (Blessed) to obtain his heavenly kingdom.

| Christ's Beatitude | Your Mindset |
|---|---|
| Blessed are the poor in spirit: for theirs is the kingdom of heaven. | Recognize we need God's rich spirit and help. The reward is Heaven. |
| Blessed are they that mourn: for they shall be comforted. | The loss of any person, thing, emotion, or finance gives a feeling of mourning. Also, when we have regrets that stem from sin, be remorseful. For those we observe morning, be prepared to provide comfort and support. |
| Blessed are the meek: for they shall inherit the earth. | Avoid being boastful and asserting one's self above others. Eliminate the human EGO (Easing God Out). God is control of all outcomes and events. |
| Blessed are they which do hunger and thirst after righteousness: for they shall be filled. | Have an intense craving for God's righteousness. God will sense the desire so that you will be more than satisfied. |
| Blessed are the merciful: for they shall obtain mercy. | Show kindness and forgiveness to others so that you will receive kindness and mercy in the event you make a mistake. |
| Blessed are the pure in heart: for they shall see God. | Pursue purity and righteousness in your thoughts and life choices so that you will be able to see God who is pure (Do what is right, when nobody and everybody is watching). |
| Blessed are the peacemakers: for they shall be called the children of God. | Be a promoter of Peace before, during, and after a conflict so that you can be called a child of God. |
| Blessed are they which are persecuted for righteousness' sake: for theirs is the kingdom of heaven. | Remain firm with your faith with God. When others attempt to ridicule or punish you because you are doing what is right. |

| Christ's Beatitude | Your Mindset |
| --- | --- |
| Blessed are ye, when men shall revile you, and persecute you, and shall say all manner of evil against you falsely, | Be prepared and react in a positive God-like manner when people disparage you by making false statements. |
| Rejoice and be glad, because great is your reward in heaven, for in the same way they persecuted the prophets who were before you. | Remember, God's prophets came and told the people the truth, even if it hurt. Always hold fast to the truth in the face of adversity, because heaven is your reward. There are evil forces formed through people to oppose God's truth and to keep you from your reward. |

# Chapter 5 – Free Will – God's Gift

Many preachers, teachers, and scholars claim that the present day is a present (gift) from God. The question is, "Are you making good use of your present?" The answer you give can be two-fold concerning, good use of your life and good use of your time.

If you're not sure of your answer, it is deemed that you are not making good use of your life and time. Ask yourself, "Would you waste your favorite meal?" Chances are you would be sure if you finished your favorite meal and how good it was, you would never be uncertain in this area. To add, you would be infuriated (angry) to see someone take one taste of your favorite meal and throw it away while cursing it. Another scenario, a person who would just let what you consider an excellent meal sit on their lap without taking one taste, then throwing it away without a thought.

Well, the same holds when you wake up every morning and decide to be bitter and angry, or when you choose to sit idle all day in front of a TV watching others live fake lives to entertain you. In a way, it's similar to you or anyone wasting your favorite meal. There are so many gifts provided by God, and in no way could be limited by these listed items:

1. The gift of Time and Consciousness
2. The gift of Salvation provided by Christ
3. The gift of the Holy Ghost (Comforter)
4. The gift of Free Will and Choice

To make choices and to deal with the consequences (results), either good or bad, is living life. In everyday life, we're confronted by choices either small or big concerning what we engage in, such as thoughts, reading, eating, drinking, attitude, friends, places, spending, speaking, pleasures, actions, reactions, etc.…

To put what you read in Chapter 3 into practice, wake up each morning thankful for the gift of salvation provided by Christ, and recite (repeat) all the Commandments. Then close at night by reflecting on your day and if you lived up to what God expects of you. For example, did you steal from your employer or your school? Think hard on this subject because many of us do, it does not have to be material things we are stealing. However, it could be several acts or inactions. For example, we goofed off at work, procrastinated (delay) at handling assignments, or did not give our teacher the proper attention to learning something new (i.e., stealing from your employer when you don't implement tasks required of you and not paying attention in school can only lead to stealing from yourself); that my friend is stealing.

To "not" steal in this aspect, you will see your life excel. Meaning your teacher, boss, and co-workers will recognize your work ethic; you will open up more opportunities for yourself.

When making choices, you're exercising your gift of *free will* even if the options are force-of-habits. God's order can become a force of good habit. Once again, start every day with remembering Christ's salvation and God's commandments and close every evening by reflecting on your day. If you realize any violations, ask God's forgiveness. If you offended anyone and did not seek their forgiveness after the offense, do your best to apologize the next time you see that person.

I learned from several influential (powerful) speakers that your emotions are choices… like choosing to wake up and have a great day. If you plan it in your heart and mind to have a great day, you will have a great day (Even if someone offends you or tries to steal your joy). By making up your mind before you get out of bed in the morning, you can deflect any negative attempts like an annoying mosquito.

However, when you are easily agitated (annoyed) your mindset dwells on any offense, and you will tend to react negatively; that within itself gives the other person the power. Don't be trapped, do your best to anticipate (predict) without dwelling on the types of offenses to control your reaction to the same. If you think for a brief moment, before starting your day, you could probably predict 90 percent of the offenses you might encounter. So by planning, you may be able to identify future daily offenses and who may be the offending party. There are some surprises, and you can't forecast them all, but I'm sure you could train your mind to react positively… and to hold your silence (it is usually stronger than an outburst of rage).

In keeping with the spirit of living life and making good choices, the opposite of this is idleness. To sit around and do nothing is a waste of life. If you choose to be upset with anything, get upset when you see that you are: idle, complacent, or in previous examples - wasting your favorite dinner.

Yes, God took a day of rest from all of His labors and so should you. Does that mean to remain in a vegetative (plant-like) state on the couch watching TV or playing Video Games…? No. Make use of your time and read your Bible and a book. Reflect on things that could be of service to God and others. Think of strategies and forecast how you can avoid adverse actions and reactions that will occur in your lifetime.

Beware of people and things that attempt to control your free will, or shall we say those who try to enslave you: spiritually, mentally, physically, socially and financially (I'll expand on these five issues later). Yes, there are forces out there that try to control your life and manipulate (control) you to do things for their benefit without giving back.

Based on those who want to control you for their purpose it is essential to know who you are and what you want out of life. It is scary to hear young people and even adults say, "I'm trying to find myself…." That alone is concerning because if you don't know who you are, you are easy to manipulate. Anyone with a silver tongue of compliments or sadistically dogmatic (cruelly strict) can mold you into what they want you to be, instead of what you need and want to be. In essence, before engaging the world and leaving the nest, know who you are. If you profess (confess) God to be the head of your life, then you already know the answer.

Previously mentioned are several ways which others may try to control and manipulate you. Well, the first one I mentioned is spiritual control. You'll find most of this taking place where there are extreme (strict) religious institutions. If you can remember a Reverend by the name of Jim Jones; he was able to get a significant amount of his congregation (audience) to commit suicide in one night. To strengthen your spirituality, know your Bible, read it for yourself. Then you will see that God has longsuffering (patient) for all of humankind and does not want to infringe upon the gifts that He has given all of us, "Free Will and Salvation." If God did not want you to live anymore in this world, He could make the appropriate arrangements for your departure. In the meantime, enjoy the gifts that God has given you by exercising your spirituality and maintaining a personal relationship with Him. Be knowledgeable of His word and seek His will (not man's will).

The next category discusses Mental Control, which occurs when people try to control your thoughts. Mental control happens just about every day, especially if you watch the news and believe every report. Yes, there are plenty of things going on in the world, and the news media does its best to consolidate it in such a short period. Based on the quick and brief work of the media there is a good chance the information you receive is fragmented (pieces), distorted (fuzzy), or not even the truth. The people reporting the news usually don't have any control on what they are communicating; they are controlled by gatekeepers behind the scenes who want to push their agenda, which may not be for the benefit of all people as a whole. That's why it is essential only to believe fifty percent of the information you see on TV and read in newspapers.

Physical control is when your human body is confined. If it is not slavery or kidnapping, it is a state of Incarceration (Jail). I like the way Hill Harper put it in his book… *"It's a matter of staying in the game."* Going to jail for a crime you committed or didn't commit, you are out of the game. Your physical being is controlled by an institution that tells you what to do: when to go to bed, take a shower, go out for recreation, when to eat, what to eat. Physical control is what we all want to avoid.

Social control is living up to the expectations of others, because of your status in life or your desire to fellowship with a particular group. To nullify (cancel) this issue, seek to live up to God's expectation of you and be involved with those who share His interest (All others are acquaintances/contacts). Christ said, *"No man can serve two masters: for either he will hate the one, and love the other; or else he will hold to the one, and despise the other. Ye cannot serve God and mammon." (Matthew 6:24 KJV)* So don't let your career, economics, or social status control you; you control it.

Last category, Finances, this is a little more direct than social control. To let your finances control your life means going into a great deal of debt by living above your means, or by working too much for money and not giving your time or tithe to God. Now, many financial planners will tell you the difference between good debt and bad debt - 99 percent of them are right. Debts related to things that appreciate (increase) or enhance your life are preferable (This is discussed more in later chapters). All other debts are, but if you must, keep it under control. Avoid going into debt for things that depreciate (decrease); like a pricey car that is way out of your means, and expensive clothing, etc.... It's nice to have beautiful items; however, if it is going to keep you in debt or away from God, reduce your expenditures (expenses) in materialistic things and give your time and tithe to God. So in essence, don't let your debt control you where it causes you to get frustrated with life and ignore God. Keep in mind, most of the items you possess will usually bore you rather quickly, and chances are it's going to wear and tear. Therefore, why waste your dreams and hopes on lesser things?

God entrust you with a priceless gift of life and time. To squander (waste) your life and time or let someone else waste it for you is a disservice to Him and the purpose He has for your life and time.

Now there are others who don't want to acknowledge God and take the gift of life and time for granted. However, there is a way to demonstrate the appreciation of God's love, by accepting His Son who came in the flesh and died for our sins so that we can have eternal life. Ephesians 2: 8 -10:

> *"For by the grace you have been saved through faith. And this is not your own doing; it is the gift of God, not a result of works, so that no one may boast. For we are His workmanship created in Christ Jesus for good works, which God prepared beforehand, that we should walk in them."(KJV)*

The Gift of salvation provided by Christ's sacrifice demonstrates God's love and desire to want to commune (connect) with us for all of eternity (time with no end). God is gracious (kind) and loving that He provides us with free will to see if we are willing to reciprocate (share); by accepting this truth and fact on our own. If in the fortunate event; you do believe that the Son of God came in the flesh, died for your sins, rose from the dead you are a child of the Most High God. Moreover, you demonstrated your belief by confessing and repenting of your sins; then being baptized as a personal proclamation (announcement) for wanting to be like Christ. Further, you are confident that Christ has left us a comforter, the Holy Spirit to guide and give us understanding. The gift of the Holy Spirit is alive and well in this world. To activate His involvement in your life requires your acknowledgment of God, the Son, and the Holy Spirit (It is just that simple).

God is giving and pours out His blessings on those He finds favor. God is kind enough to place certain gifts within every one of us. The question is, "Are you using the gifts God has given you to bless others, and edify (build on) His name?" The blessings and gifts flow down from God, but what are you doing to share the gifts God has placed in you?

Now you're wondering, "What gifts has God placed in me through the Holy Spirit?" Although, we may have unique human characteristics: artistic, creativity, intelligence, and unique gifts associated with your flesh. However, there are gifts concerning how we give praise to the Lord and help others.

In 1 Corinthians 12:27-31:

*"Now ye are the body of Christ, and members in particular. And God hath set some in the church, first apostles, secondarily prophets, thirdly teachers, after that miracles, then gifts of healings, helps, governments, diversities of tongues. Are all apostles? Are all prophets? Are all teachers? Are all workers of miracles? Have all the gifts of healing? Do all speak with tongues? Do all interpret? But covet earnestly the best gifts: and yet shew I unto you a more excellent way." (KJV)*

The gifts associated with how you give back to the body of Christ (The Church) are:

1. Prophesy – Ability to receive and deliver a message from God that can be foretelling or encouraging.
2. Service – Ability to care for the needs of the church as a whole.
3. Teaching – Ability to understand God's word and present information so that others can learn.
4. Exhortation – The ability to motivate and encourage others.
5. Giving – Ability to provide material resources in a cheerful manner.
6. Leadership – Ability to provide goals to a group to fulfill God's purpose.
7. Mercy – Ability exercise compassion and relate to those who are suffering or distressed.
8. Wisdom – Ability to address situations by following God's word that provides guidance on how to proceed or handle problems.
9. Knowledge – The ability to gather and analyze information for the benefit of others.
10. Faith – Ability to believe God's power will favorably overcome any and all circumstances.
11. Healing – Serve as an instrument of God's supernatural powers to heal those physically afflicted.
12. Miracles – Serve as an instrument of God's supernatural powers that defies the laws of physics for this world.
13. Distinguishing of Spirits – Ability to discern between true or false teaching; Identify spiritual or carnal intent which can be driven by heavenly or evil forces.
14. Tongues – The ability to receive a spiritual message in another tongue (language) that was never learned.
15. Interpretation of Tongues – Ability to translate a message spoken in tongues (language) to edify (build) the entire church.
16. Discipleship – Ability to establish new churches and lead the lost to Christ.

17. Help – Ability to aid others individually, as opposed to helping a group as defined in Service.
18. Administration – The ability to manage the day to day affairs of the church and follow through on plans.
19. Evangelism – The ability to lead non-believers toward the knowledge of Christ in a group or individually.
20. Pastors (Shepherd) – The ability to protect, lead, cultivate and care for the needs of the church. (Bible.org)

A person can have a single spiritual gift or multiple spiritual gifts. However, exercising your gifts in a Bible teaching church is the least you can do, mainly because of the gifts of "Life" and "Time" that have been bestowed upon you….

To recap:

1. Life is all about choices; make good ones according to what God expects from you.

2. Align your free will with God's will; resistance only leads to failure.

3. Your attitude dictates your success; so make up your mind and stick to your daily plan.

4. Don't waste the gifts God has given you; exercise your mind, soul, and body.

5. To let things and others control your free will is not God's plan for you.

6. Identify and exercise your spiritual gift(s).

# Chapter 6 – Sacrifice and Salvation

The idea surrounding sacrifice and salvation are closely linked when discussing Christian principles and beliefs. The Old Testament (Hebrew Canon) describes the practice of sacrifice from its origin in Judaism. The New Testament, where Christianity begins, describes the transition of sacrificial practices in the atonement of sin through Christ, which allows everyone to receive salvation and makes all things new.

According to the American Heritage College Dictionary, the definition of Sacrifice is an act of slaughtering an animal or person or surrendering a possession as an offering to God, or a divine, or supernatural figure. The definition of Salvation is preservation or deliverance from harm, ruin, or loss. The combination of sacrifice and salvation is the essence of many religious tenets (principles and beliefs). When reading the Bible, the Old Testament is filled with sacrificial practices and offerings for the atonement of sins with a goal to maintain favor with God. The New Testament presents Christ as the sacrifice and atonement for all our sins and the means for obtaining eternal life. To receive the salvation of Christ one must believe that He is the Son of the living God and risen from the dead (John 3:16). The act of baptism is a proclamation of personal faith and allegiance to Christ. It signifies a desire to be like Christ in death and resurrection, but what is most important "Believing."

## Blood Sacrifice

When Adam ate the forbidden fruit against God's instruction, Adam's descendants (everyone) received the sentence of death. The following consequences flowed from Adam's disobedience:

- Permanent exile from the Garden of Eden

- Discontinued access to the tree of life

- Lost innocence through the knowledge of good and evil

- Alienation from God when Adam refused to confess

- Assignment of blame instead of assumed responsibility

- Spiritual death and mortality

Adam and Eve knowing they were naked, God made a garment of animal skin. This implies something had to die to cover their nakedness (The fact that God didn't destroy Adam and Eve immediately demonstrates His longsuffering, mercy, and patience). The animal skin clothing serves as the first act of sacrifice to atone for humankind's sin (remission) of disobedience by the shedding of blood.

Why is Blood so important when it comes to flesh and life? Blood represents life in the flesh and God forbade drinking it. That is why the thought and practice of vampires is an abomination.

> *And whatsoever man there be of the children of Israel, or of the strangers that sojourn among you, which hunteth and catcheth any beast or fowl that may be eaten; he shall even pour out the blood thereof, and cover it with dust. For it is the life of all flesh; the blood of it is for the life thereof: therefore I said unto the children of Israel, Ye shall eat the blood of no manner of flesh: for the life of all flesh is the blood thereof: whosoever eateth it shall be cut off (Leviticus 17:13-14 KJV).*

> *Only be sure that thou eat not the blood: for the blood is the life; and thou mayest not eat the life with the flesh (Deuteronomy 12:23 KJV).*

Additional acts of sacrifice are outlined throughout the Old Testament through various offerings of grains, oils, and animals: Bull, Ox, Sheep, Ram, Goats, Pigeon, and Dove. For example, you can find references to the following types of offerings:

Burnt: general devotion to God
Grain: voluntary devotion for God's provision
Peace: treaties made before God
Sin: purification from sin before going to God
Trespass: debt owed because of damages to another person

When looking at the fourth-dimensional view (time), Adam brought sin into the world and disrupted the peaceful order through his disobedience. God gave Adam dominion over the earth (land, sea, and air). Consequently, all things including Adam's bloodline were tainted and humankind inherited sin and death. Adam's act of disobedience corrupted his bloodline, and everyone born through his seed (sperm) will inherit that impurity (man and woman).

God, the epitome of integrity through his living word set the rules and natural order for women to give birth to children (Genesis 3:16). Moreover, the Lord made a prophetic declaration of complete redemption for Adam and Eve even after they defied Him, and it applies to all their descendants:

So the Lord God said to the serpent,

*"Because you have done this, Cursed are you above all livestock and all wild animals! You will crawl on your belly, and you will eat dust all the days of your life. And I will put enmity between you and the woman, and between your offspring[a] and hers; he will crush[b] your head, and you will strike his heel." To the woman, he said, "I will make your pains in childbearing very severe; with painful labor you will give birth to children. Your desire will be for your husband, and he will rule over you." (Genesis 3:14-16 KJV)*

In these scriptures, God addresses the serpent and Satan. Without knowing the original form of the serpent, it was reformed to crawl on the ground because of God's word and judgment. The portion of the verse that addresses Satan is the statement of enmity (hostility) between good and evil. The offspring of Satan are unredeemed people and spirits who enjoy doing evil. The woman's seed (egg), the union between the Virgin Mary and the Holy Spirit, is Christ and those who believe in Him.

Since man's blood was tainted by disobedience in the garden, it is no longer pure. Furthermore, man had dominion over the earth; therefore, all manner of life (animals and nature) became tainted/corrupt along with man's blood.

God the Father, Christ the Son, and the Holy Spirit are pure. Their presence and existence can make anything pure. An example used earlier, human beings moved by the Holy Spirit wrote the Bible. Many would argue that human beings are fallible; therefore, the Bible is prone to error. Nevertheless, when the Holy Spirit inspires someone, that divine act overrides the human flaw and perfects the result: the Bible. In essence, when God is in it, what He touches becomes perfect.

God planned for the perfect union between the Holy Spirit and the woman's seed (egg) while removing the corrupt seed of man from the equation (Genesis 3:15, Matthew 1:20). The Holy Spirit planted a spiritual seed in Mary that Created God's son, Jesus Christ (Luke 1:35):

> *"And the angel answered and said unto her, The Holy Ghost shall come upon thee, and the power of the Highest shall overshadow thee: therefore also that holy thing which shall be born of thee shall be called the Son of God." (KJV)*

Christ bloodline was not from Adam, like the rest of us. In addition, Christ walked the earth in the flesh but without sin or corruption. He willingly came into this world and gave his life as a pure sacrifice (Hebrews 10). Ultimately, Jesus could have called a legion of angels to end His suffering, but he endured the whole of it to secure redemption and eternal life for everyone (Matthew 25:53).

The expression that the serpent, Satan, would bruise His heal symbolizes the evil that would crucify Christ and challenge God's children. However, crushing the serpent's head professes the victory Christ has over the head of evil. Jesus' pureblood, freedom from sin, willingness to die and resurrection demonstrates his victory over sin and death. Jesus' sacrifice was the only means for saving the children of Adam and Eve from this fallen world and giving them access to eternal life. Christ's willing sacrifice makes the payment of sin possible. God, in His grace, will forgive anyone who "Believes" Jesus is the Son of God and that He arose from the dead.

So why did Christ have to suffer and encounter this turmoil? Again, the Biblical precedent and prophetic statement are found in Genesis 3:15 (see table). God would be willing to sacrifice His own Son to redeem man, but would man be willing to sacrifice his son for a relationship with God? The act of reciprocity (mutual benefit) was the foundation where God patiently waited for a faithful man and tested him. The man found to be faithful was Abraham. God tested him by requesting that he sacrifice his promised son, Isaac (who he waited one hundred years until he was born). Abraham was determined to follow through on God's request; however, an Angel had to call Abraham's name twice to get his attention to stop him from following through on sacrificing his son (Genesis 22:1-19). God never favored the practice of sacrificing children. God rewarded Abraham's obedience and willingness to sacrifice Isaac with a blessing that flows to all his descendants. This act set the stage for everyone's redemption. Abraham did not have to sacrifice his son, whose bloodline comes from Adam (carries the promise of death and remains contaminated). God sent his own Son through a new bloodline that was pure, spiritual and free from corruption to a virgin named, Mary - the seed (egg) of the woman and descendant of Abraham.

God's son was the pure sacrifice His blood remains incorruptible and sufficient to gain eternal life. The promise made to Abraham and his descendants for his act of obedience is officially transferred to all nations/people through Christ's sacrifice.

*And in thy seed shall all the nations of the earth be blessed; because thou hast obeyed my voice. (Genesis 22:18 KJV)*

*That the blessing of Abraham might come on the Gentiles through Jesus Christ; that we might receive the promise of the Spirit through faith. (Galatians 3:14 KJV)*

The ancient prophecies in the Old Testament remain vital because they foretell the coming of Christ. The Old Testament anticipated the birth of Christ, the life He lived, and the sacrifice He made of Himself centuries before these events unfolded. The New Testament (KJV) put the fulfillment of these prophecies in perspective:

| Prophecy | Fulfillment |
| --- | --- |
| Genesis 3:15<br><br>*And I will put enmity between you and the woman, and between your offspring and hers; he will crush[b] your head, and you will strike his heel.* | Matthew 1:20<br><br>*But while he thought on these things, behold, the angel of the Lord appeared unto him in a dream, saying, Joseph, thou son of David, fear not to take unto thee Mary thy wife: for that which is conceived in her is of the Holy Ghost.* |
| Isaiah 7:14<br><br>*Therefore the Lord himself shall give you a sign; Behold, a virgin shall conceive, and bear a son, and shall call his name Immanuel.* | Matthew 1:23<br><br>*Behold, a virgin shall be with child, and shall bring forth a son, and they shall call his name Emmanuel, which being interpreted is, God with us.* |
| Psalms 2:7<br><br>*I will declare the decree: the LORD hath said unto me, Thou art my Son; this day have I begotten thee.* | Matthew 3:16-17<br><br>*And Jesus, when he was baptized, went up straightway out of the water: and, lo, the heavens were opened unto him, and he saw the Spirit of God descending like a dove, and lighting upon him: And lo a voice from heaven, saying, This is my beloved Son, in whom I am well pleased.* |

| Prophecy | Fulfillment |
|---|---|
| Isaiah 61:1-2<br><br>*The Spirit of the Lord GOD is upon me; because the LORD hath anointed me to preach good tidings unto the meek; he hath sent me to bind up the brokenhearted, to proclaim liberty to the captives, and the opening of the prison to them that are bound; To proclaim the acceptable year of the LORD, and the day of vengeance of our God; to comfort all that mourn;* | Luke 4:18 19<br><br>*The Spirit of the Lord is upon me, because he hath anointed me to preach the gospel to the poor; he hath sent me to heal the brokenhearted, to preach deliverance to the captives, and recovering of sight to the blind, to set at liberty them that are bruised, To preach the acceptable year of the Lord.* |
| Psalms 110:4<br><br>*The LORD hath sworn, and will not repent, Thou art a priest for ever after the order of Melchizedek.* | Hebrew 5:5-6<br><br>*So also Christ glorified not himself to be made an high priest; but he that said unto him, Thou art my Son, today have I begotten thee. As he saith also in another place, Thou art a priest for ever after the order of Melchisedec.* |
| Psalms 35:11<br><br>*False witnesses did rise up; they laid to my charge things that I knew not.* | Mark 14:57-58<br><br>*And there arose certain, and bare false witness against him, saying, We heard him say, I will destroy this temple that is made with hands, and within three days I will build another made without hands.* |

| Prophecy | Fulfillment |
| --- | --- |
| Isaiah 53:7<br><br>*He was oppressed, and he was afflicted, yet he opened not his mouth: he is brought as a lamb to the slaughter, and as a sheep before her shearers is dumb, so he openeth not his mouth.* | Mark 15:4-5<br><br>*And Pilate asked him again, saying, Answerest thou nothing? Behold how many things they witness against thee. But Jesus yet answered nothing; so that Pilate marveled.* |
| Isaiah 53:12<br><br>*Therefore will I divide him a portion with the great, and he shall divide the spoil with the strong; because he hath poured out his soul unto death: and he was numbered with the transgressors; and he bare the sin of many, and made intercession for the transgressors.* | Matthew 27:38<br><br>*Then were there two thieves crucified with him, one on the right hand, and another on the left. Mark 15:27-28 And with him they crucify two thieves; the one on his right hand, and the other on his left. And the scripture was fulfilled, which said, And he was numbered with the transgressors.* |

| Prophecy | Fulfillment |
| --- | --- |
| Psalm 16:10<br><br>*For thou wilt not leave my soul in hell; neither wilt thou suffer thine Holy One to see corruption.*<br><br>*Psalm 49:15 But God will redeem my soul from the power of the grave: for he shall receive me. Selah.* | Matthew 28:5-7<br><br>*And the angel answered and said unto the women, Fear not ye: for I know that ye seek Jesus, which was crucified. He is not here: for he is risen, as he said. Come, see the place where the Lord lay. And go quickly, and tell his disciples that he is risen from the dead; and, behold, he goeth before you into Galilee; there shall ye see him: lo, I have told you.*<br><br>*Acts 2:30-32 Therefore being a prophet, and knowing that God had sworn with an oath to him, that of the fruit of his loins, according to the flesh, he would raise up Christ to sit on his throne; He seeing this before spake of the resurrection of Christ, that his soul was not left in hell, neither his flesh did see corruption. This Jesus hath God raised up, whereof we all are witnesses.* |

| Prophecy | Fulfillment |
|---|---|
| Isaiah 53:5-11 | Romans 5:6-8 |
| *But he was wounded for our transgressions, he was bruised for our iniquities: the chastisement of our peace was upon him; and with his stripes we are healed. All we like sheep have gone astray; we have turned everyone to his own way; and the Lord hath laid on him the iniquity of us all. He was oppressed, and he was afflicted, yet he opened not his mouth: he is brought as a lamb to the slaughter, and as a sheep before her shearers is dumb, so he openeth not his mouth. He was taken from prison and from judgment: and who shall declare his generation? For he was cut off out of the land of the living: for the transgression of my people was he stricken. And he made his grave with the wicked, and with the rich in his death; because he had done no violence, neither was any deceit in his mouth. Yet, it pleased the Lord to bruise him; he hath put him to grief: when thou shalt make his soul an offering for sin, he shall see his seed, he shall prolong his days, and the pleasure of the Lord shall prosper in his hand. He shall see of the travail of his soul, and shall be satisfied: by his knowledge shall my righteous servant justify many; for he shall bear their iniquities.* | *For when we were yet without strength, in due time Christ died for the ungodly. For scarcely for a righteous man will one die: yet peradventure for a good man some would even dare to die. But God commendeth his love toward us, in that, while we were yet sinners, Christ died for us.* |

Reference: https://www.thoughtco.com/prophecies-of-jesus-fulfilled

Christ's blood was pure and free from the curse of death brought into the world by Adam. Believers should act on their faith and be baptized to show their allegiance to God. The life a person lives after professing their faith should be a testament to all.

The curse brought by Adam condemned our earthly bodies to death, but what about our souls (the energy that gives us consciousness and our inner voice)? 1 Corinthians Chapter 15:40-50 provides the answer:

> *There are also bodies in the heavens and bodies on the earth. The glory of the heavenly bodies is different from the glory of the earthly bodies. The sun has one kind of glory, while the moon and stars each have another kind. And even the stars differ from each other in their glory. It is the same way with the resurrection of the dead. Our earthly bodies are planted in the ground when we die, but they will be raised to live forever. Our bodies are buried in brokenness, but they will be raised in glory. They are buried in weakness, but they will be raised in strength. They are buried as natural human bodies, but they will be raised as spiritual bodies. For just as there are natural bodies, there are also spiritual bodies. The Scriptures tell us, "The first man, Adam, became a living person."[a] But the last Adam—that is, Christ—is a life-giving Spirit. What comes first is the natural body, then the spiritual body comes later. Adam, the first man, was made from the dust of the earth, while Christ, the second man, came from heaven. Earthly people are like the earthly man, and heavenly people are like the heavenly man. Just as we are now like the earthly man, we will someday be like[b] the heavenly man. What I am saying, dear brothers and sisters, is that our physical bodies cannot inherit the Kingdom of God. These dying bodies cannot inherit what will last forever. (KJV)*

Revelations 2:10-11:

> *Fear none of those things which thou shalt suffer: behold, the devil shall cast some of you into prison, that ye may be tried; and ye shall have tribulation ten days: be thou faithful unto death, and I will give thee a crown of life. He that hath an ear, let him hear what the Spirit saith unto the churches; He that overcometh shall not be hurt of the second death. (KJV)*

Hebrews 10:5-7

> *Therefore, when Christ came into the world, he said: "Sacrifice and offering you did not desire, but a body you prepared for me; with burnt offerings and*

*sin offerings you were not pleased. Then I said, 'Here I am—it is written about me in the scroll— I have come to do your will, my God.'" (KJV)*

Christ came into the world with pure blood borne of the union between the Virgin Mary and the Holy Spirit. Through His blood the sacrifice of animals is no longer needed; the atonement and forgiveness of sins can be made. The laws surrounding dietary practices outlined in the Old Testament are also in the New Testament:

*Mark 16:18 They shall take up serpents; and if they drink any deadly thing, it shall not hurt them; they shall lay hands on the sick, and they shall recover. (KJV)*

*Mark 7:18 – 20 And he saith unto them, Are ye so without understanding also? Do ye not perceive, that whatsoever thing from without entereth into the man, it cannot defile him; Because it entereth not into his heart, but into the belly, and goeth out into the draught, purging all meats? And he said, That which cometh out of the man, that defileth the man. For from within, out of the heart of men, proceed evil thoughts, adulteries, fornications, murders, Thefts, covetousness, wickedness, deceit, lasciviousness, an evil eye, blasphemy, pride, foolishness: All these evil things come from within, and defile the man. (KJV)*

To fully appreciate the salvation Christ provided for everyone, understanding the full extent of His Sacrifice remains essential. He came and lived a sin-free life for approximately 33 years. He was falsely accused, bitterly persecuted, and willingly died on the cross without blemish. His pure blood serves as the atonement for all sin: a debt for which no child born of Adam or any beast on Earth could ever satisfy.

## **Overview:**

1. Adam had dominion over this world and through his disobedience created a fallen/sinful state.

2. God covered Adam and Eve's nakedness with the skin of an animal He sacrificed for their sin.

3. God tested Abraham to see if he would sacrifice his promised son, Isaac – but stopped him from completing the act.

4. God sacrificed his son for the remission of all sin, creating a New Covenant.

5. Jesus' coming into the world was foretold in the Old Testament.

6. Jesus Blood was spiritually pure from the Holy Spirit and the Virgin Mary.

7. Christ's passion was to return man to God for the new heaven and earth to come.

8. Because of Christ's blood, we can wash away our sins and stand in the pure presence of God.

9. Christ rising from the dead shows, He is free from the curse of death brought into the world by Adam.

10. Through Christ's sacrifice, all things are made new.

## Old Testament

- ➢ Israelites offered sacrifices to gain favor and a good relationship with God.

- ➢ Types of Sacrifice: oxen, bulls, rams, goats, lambs, grain, oil, and flour.

- ➢ Moses delivered the Ten Commandments.

- ➢ Priests provided dietary requirements for themselves and the congregation.

- ➢ The Law of Moses identified the circumstances that would render a person ritually impure.

## New Testament

- Everyone has an opportunity to gain citizenship in God's new kingdom to come.

- Jesus Christ is the pure and ultimate sacrifice. Thus eliminating the need to offer animals, vegetation, or material items.

- Jesus issues two commandments that sum up the Ten Commandments.

- Jesus repeals dietary restrictions: What defiles a man is what he speaks and does, not what goes into his stomach.

- All things are made clean because of the sacrifice of Christ.

- It is not the Law **_or_** Grace; it is the Law **_and_** Grace.

Benefits of Christ:

| Old Testament Offering | Scripture | New Testament | Christ's Nature |
|---|---|---|---|
| Burnt | Leviticus 1:3-17; 6:8-13 | Compensation and Atonement | Life without Sin |
| Grain | Leviticus 2:1-16; 6:14-23 | Loyalty and Blessing | Submissive to God's will |
| Peace | Leviticus 3:1-17; 7:11-36 | Understanding and Friendship | Peace with God |
| Sin | Leviticus 4:1-5:13; 6:24-30 | Pacification and Calming | Replacement for Death |
| Trespass | Leviticus 7:1-10 | Regret and Remorse | Complete Redemption |

# Chapter 7 – Is Your Heart Aligned with Heaven or Hell?

Having a relationship with God is a matter of the Heart. Meaning, the acts, reactions, emotions, and feelings you exhibit at any given time can determine if your heart is aligned with God. For those of you that are technical and most likely thinking, the heart is one of the strongest muscle in one's body that provides blood flow throughout the body. The involuntary beats of your heart continue to work, even while you sleep. What causes the heart to beat is the bio-electricity that every one of us holds.

Now, what does that have to do with God? Simple, Everything! God operates at multiple dimensions; some are known and unknown to man. However, the physical aspect of the heart is what He created, but gave man/woman more when He gave us a heart and mind to make choices to exercise our free will. The difference behind the heart and mind have a nuance (slight variation), the mind makes a logical choice based on certain pieces of evidence or lessons learned. While the heart is the motive behind your choices; driving your mind's thought process.

An example of the mind at work, you determine that you want to eat a particular type of food. Therefore your mind makes the rational decision for you to prepare or go out to the restaurant of your choosing. However, what is the drive behind your choice? It runs deeper when it is a matter of the Heart, it a matter of how you feel that drives your rationale (mind) to satisfy your desire.

Here is an exercise to get you in touch with your heart. For example, someone you are acquainted with gets a new job, promotion, car, or house. Seeing them with a new position or items makes you feel: jealous, envious, angry, or happy? Whatever choice you made, can be deemed as you getting in touch with your heart. Meaning the feelings you exhibit that drives your thinking.

God seeks individuals who have: a heart (desire) to be obedient, provide service to others, respects authority, truthful, and understanding. An excellent location to solidify (set) this is found in the book of Samuel, where God revokes King Saul's divine (Godly) authority over Israel, and it transfers to David through Samuel the Prophet. 1 Samuel 13:14:

> *"But now thy kingdom shall not continue: the Lord hath sought him a man after his own heart, and the Lord hath commanded him to be captain over his people, because though hast not kept that which the Lord commanded thee." (KJV)*

You are probably thinking, "What is the heart of God like? Well a brief, but un-limiting synopsis can be found in Psalms 86:15:

> *"But thou, O Lord, art a God full of compassion, and gracious, longsuffering, and plenteous in mercy and truth." (KJV)*

1. If your heart is not compassionate for others, your heart is not aligned with God.

2. If your heart is not gracious (kind), your heart is not aligned with God.

3. If your heart does not demonstrate longsuffering (tolerant and patient), your heart is not aligned with God.

4. If your heart is not full of mercy (forgiveness), your heart is not aligned with God.

5. If your heart is not full of truth, your heart is not aligned with God.

Your heart's alignment in this lifetime is an excellent trajectory into your after-life. God intended for man not to have to go through death, but what separated us from God (as expressed in Chapter 6) was the sin of Adam (Eating the forbidden fruit) and not taking ownership of it. As a result of Adam exercising his free-will, he challenged God's word through his disobedience, which was the promise of death. However, through Christ serving as the last pure sacrifice for the sins of all men, we can be resurrected by the grace He provided into the afterlife.

After one's earthly body expires, there are a few States that need to be identified. NO, not the states within the United States, but the State of consciousness (aware) or unconsciousness (unaware) one will experience when their body returns to the earth. The first State is considered a state of rest/sleep, the second is the state of Hell, and last the state of Heaven.

The State of rest/sleep without the body falls under the category of unconsciousness; this is where: one does not know who they are, where they are, or know anything about existing, living, or dying. Does a person dream after their body expires (Not able to answer that question)? However, a close example that helps to bring biblical light to rest/sleep after death is found in 1 Samuel 28:7-20:

> *Then said Saul unto his servants, Seek me a woman that hath a familiar spirit, that I may go to her, and enquire of her. And his servants said to him, Behold, there is a woman that hath a familiar spirit at Endor. And Saul disguised himself, and put on other raiment, and he went, and two men with him, and they came to the woman by night: and he said, I pray thee, divine unto me by the familiar spirit, and bring me him up, whom I shall name unto thee. And the woman said unto him, Behold, thou knowest what Saul hath done, how he hath cut off those that have familiar spirits, and the wizards, out of the land: wherefore then layest thou a snare for my life, to cause me to die? And Saul sware to her by the Lord, saying, As the Lord liveth, there shall no punishment happen to thee for this thing. Then said the woman, Whom shall*

*I bring up unto thee? And he said, Bring me up Samuel. And when the woman saw Samuel, she cried with a loud voice: and the woman spake to Saul, saying, Why hast thou deceived me? for thou art Saul. And the king said unto her, Be not afraid: for what sawest thou? And the woman said unto Saul, I saw gods ascending out of the earth. And he said unto her, What form is he of? And she said, An old man cometh up; and he is covered with a mantle. And Saul perceived that it was Samuel, and he stooped with his face to the ground, and bowed himself. And Samuel said to Saul, Why hast thou disquieted me, to bring me up? And Saul answered, I am sore distressed; for the Philistines make war against me, and God is departed from me, and answereth me no more, neither by prophets, nor by dreams: therefore I have called thee, that thou mayest make known unto me what I shall do. Then said Samuel, Wherefore then dost thou ask of me, seeing the Lord is departed from thee, and is become thine enemy? And the Lord hath done to him, as he spake by me: for the Lord hath rent the kingdom out of thine hand, and given it to thy neighbour, even to David: Because thou obeyedst not the voice of the Lord, nor executedst his fierce wrath upon Amalek, therefore hath the Lord done this thing unto thee this day. Moreover the Lord will also deliver Israel with thee into the hand of the Philistines: and tomorrow shalt thou and thy sons be with me: the Lord also shall deliver the host of Israel into the hand of the Philistines. (KJV)*

Israel's first King, Saul, lowered himself by disobeying God. As a result, he fell from God's grace and favor. He sought a medium (humans who can talk to the dead); which God forbids, along with soothsayers (fortune tellers), and astrologers (people who read the stars and zodiac signs). In Deuteronomy 18:9-12:

> *When you come into the land that the Lord your God is giving you, you shall not learn to follow the abominable practices of those nations. There shall not be found among you anyone who burns his son or his daughter as an offering, anyone who practices divination or tells fortunes or interprets omens, or a sorcerer or a charmer or a medium or a necromancer or one who inquires of the*

*dead, for whoever does these things is an abomination to the Lord. And because of these abominations the Lord your God is driving them out before you. (KJV)*

The idea of consulting and looking for answers from individuals with this ability takes your focus away from Almighty God Himself, who can change any circumstance. The placing of one's trust in what they hear from people with this ability is another test of your free-will, on whether you will choose to trust in the Lord through prayer, or in evil spirits through these charmers (?). Keep in mind if a fortune teller could tell the future, we would have a great deal of lottery winning fortune tellers.

Now the State of consciousness has a level of awareness of existing, but most importantly, a State of awareness concerning one's surroundings and interactions. Heaven and Hell are both States. Once again, not like Nebraska, Texas, New York or California, etc....

To start on the negative then end on the positive; Hell is a State of Consciousness that is overwhelmed with a feeling of uncaring, rude, impatient, unforgiving, and false delusions. The state of Hell breeds misery, greed, pain, fear, suffering, and torment. Ultimately Hell produces an un-ending conclusion of fire and brimstone prepared for the devil and his angels *(Matthew 25:41 KJV)*.

WOW!!! The questions one should be asking:

1. Is my heart aligned with Hell?

2. Does my Heart (desire) take pleasure in others suffering?

3. Am I rude to people and act impatient?

4. Do I have an unforgiving heart and harbor offenses caused by others either accidentally or intentionally?

5. Do I partake in bearing false information and enjoy misleading people?

If your answer to one of these questions is yes, your trajectory is aligned with Hell. Now, if you will go there remains with God.

Now let's get on the positive track, Heaven. Heaven is that wonderful state we all strive for, where God's glory shines on its inhabitants continuously. To give you that euphoric (joyful) sense of Heaven: every minute is like the Super Bowl where everyone scores a touchdown; the World Series and hitting a home run; or the NBA finals and you hit the last shot at the Buzzer. Wait a minute, Nah! It's 1 Billion times better than the description presented.

Heaven is a state where the citizens are caring and kind to one another. They are in no rush to go somewhere because they are in the place they need to be. The idea of mercy and forgiveness is passed away because there are no more offenses. The truth of where you are and how you bask (relax) in God's glory endures forever.

Based on the wonderful description of Heaven, the questions one should be asking, "Is my Heart aligned with Heaven?"

1. Does my Heart take pleasure in others success and happiness?

2. Am I kind to those who are nice and mean to me by acting and reacting in a God-like manner?

3. Do I practice patience for others?

4. Do I have a heart ready to forgive those who accidentally or intentionally cause injury?

5. Do I seek the truth in all matters and understand that there is more than one side to a story?

6. Do you believe in God, His Son, and the Holy Spirit?

If you answered "No" to any of the questions, your heart's trajectory is not aligned with Heaven. Your entry into the eternal

Kingdom of God may be in question, but the decision remains with the Most High.

Where you spend eternity depends on the choices you make as you exercise your free-will on earth. Keep in mind there are evil spirits that come off as light to confuse you, and to get you to think they know better than God. Your time on earth is but a short time and 1 Peter 1:24-25 states:

> *For all flesh is as grass, and all the glory of man as the flower of grass. The grass withereth, and the flower thereof falleth away: But the word of the Lord endureth for ever. And this is the word which by the gospel is preached unto you. (KJV)*

What you do in your lifetime will require an account and final judgment. If you will bask in God's glory or burn in a lake of torment that will be filled with thoughts of your unrighteous decisions remains with the Most High. Consider the bullet that rests inside of a gun, when it's fired where was it aimed, or what was its trajectory when it departed the chamber. Take the same analogy and apply it to your life. Your heart dictates where the gun is aimed; when it's time for you to leave this earth (body - the chamber), where was your trajectory (heart) pointing, Heaven or Hell?

To go even deeper into when and where Heaven should be found, Jesus expresses in Luke 19:20-21:

> *And when he was demanded of the Pharisees, when the kingdom of God should come, he answered them and said, The kingdom of God cometh not with observation: Neither shall they say, Lo here! or, lo there! for, behold, the kingdom of God is within you. (KJV)*

A good quote made by Thomas Hardy, *"The main object of religion is not to get a man into heaven, but to get heaven into man."* That is a wonderful quote that gives some insight on how you should be ready to be transported to Heaven when it is time for your departure. Your eulogy can be easily explained, he/she was a person aligned for Heaven because they brought Heaven on Earth through their actions and reactions. They truly knew the directions to Heaven which is: *"Turn Right and Keep Straight"* Anonymous.

Things to take away from this Chapter:

1. What is the state of your Heart (Desire)?

2. Having a relationship with God is a heart condition. Are you conditioning your heart to align with God?

3. Ask yourself every day, "Am I aligned with Heaven or Hell?"

4. The opportunities to bring Heaven or Hell on earth are all around you, what state are you magnifying?

5. No man/woman can place you in Heaven or Hell.

6. God is the ultimate Judge. What will you hear on your judgment day? *"And then will I profess unto them, I never knew you: depart from me, ye that work iniquity." (Matthew 7:23 KJV)* Or, *"Here is the patience of the saints: here are they that keep the commandments of God, and the faith of Jesus." (Revelation 14:12 KJV)*

# Chapter 8 – Dark Forces

During your time on this earth, there are forces that exist whose job is to counter God and His purposes, even though their bitter end will be defeated. The reality of being on God's team is you already won. God's team is going to win no matter what good or bad thing occurs in this lifetime. The most challenging question is, how does one identify an opposing team member when your job is to love everyone no matter what or even when they hate you (Matthew 5:44-46).

> *"But I say unto you, Love your enemies, bless them that curse you, do good to them that hate you, and pray for them which despitefully use you, and persecute you. That ye may be the children of your Father which is in heaven: for he maketh his sun to rise on the evil and on the good, and sendeth rain on the just and on the unjust. For if ye love them which love you, what reward have ye? do not even the publicans the same?" (KJV)*

WOW!!! This can be quite confusing (???). Well, to unravel what seems to be a riddle, all humans are made up of three things: Flesh, Soul, & Spirit. The Flesh seeks the craving of this world (Greed, Sex, Strife, Sin, etc...). The Spirit seeks a relationship with God and is pure. The Soul is the battleground where your heart and mind exercises its God-given free-will and makes choices. The only question people must ask themselves are your choices driven by Flesh or by Spirit (keep in mind the two cannot reside together)? In essence, people are driven by the spirit or the flesh. Determining if their choices and actions are good or bad is for God to judge, but for you to be aware. You must remain in the Spirit by demonstrating love. To stoop to a lower level (which is the flesh) and counter negative behavior with negative behavior only keeps strife ongoing. The main idea is to separate the negative person from their actions and reactions. Reason being, as long as they are living on this earth, they have been granted the privilege of receiving forgiveness through the ultimate sacrifice of Jesus Christ. With a new pledge of allegiance all your sins are forgiven by God; however, the only sin that will not be forgiven is blasphemy (cursing God's name/work) against the Holy Spirit.

To give clarity when dealing with people, "Love the person, but not the Sin." Meaning you should not allow negative actions or reactions spin you down a negative path where corrupt things and cursing come out of your mouth. All that you speak should be for the edification (building) of God's Kingdom toward others and yourself. To simplify it more, if you plant an apple seed in the ground, the apple seed will grow into an apple tree over time that will multiply into more apples in due season. God's power is an increasing power that is about multiplication/exponential. Therefore, planting good seeds of encouragement with your mouth can only breed good things in due season, as opposed to planting corrupt and harmful words of negativity that can only grow negativity in due season.

Another force that exists with a goal to steal your faith in God is found in Leviticus 20:6 & Deuteronomy 18:10.

> *"And the soul that turneth after such as have familiar spirits, and after wizards, to go a whoring after them, I will even set my face against that soul, and will cut him off from among his people." (KJV)*

> *"There shall not be found among you any one that maketh his son or his daughter to pass through the fire, or that useth divination, or an observer of times, or an enchanter, or a witch." (KJV)*

When a person exercises their free will to go after people with familiar spirits (communicates with the dead), wizards, witches, enchanters, and observer of times, their faith is not aligned with God. Although these forces exist, they have limited power and foresight over God. As expressed before, imagine if a fortune-teller could give you the lottery numbers, we would have a lot more lottery winners in America (???). Once again bringing back into scope, why seek advice from a losing team, instead of just being on God's team.

Looking for answers about your life through fortune telling is not living your life under God's plan. Every day, you should be seeking guidance from God the creator of it all and controller of all life. To consult with another creation instead of the creator is an insult. Live your life by the spirit, so that God's will can shine through you.

Here is a little test question for you to ask yourself, to see what channel your life is on. Do you enjoy horror movies or scary movies and take pleasure in watching others get hurt or scared? If you do enjoy these types of film, be mindful that the movie is designed to instill the spirit of fear and to propagate evil spirits to occupy your mind/soul. As a result, your focus and faith may not be on God who is the sovereign authority of all dimensions. Therefore, don't give your energy and time to wicked depictions/fears that lead to evil thoughts that may negatively influence the choices you make in life.

Ephesians 2:2-3 expresses:

> *"Wherein in time past ye walked according to the course of this world, according to the prince of the power of the air, the spirit that now worketh in the children of disobedience: Among whom also we all had our conversation in times past in the lusts of our flesh, fulfilling the desires of the flesh and of the mind; and were by nature the children of wrath, even as others."(KJV)*

One of the first documented words God spoke can be found in Genesis Chapter 1 verse 3: "And God said, Let there be light: and there was light." In the New Testament, scriptures that augment and expand on the benefits of "Light" found in John Chapter 1: 1-9:

> *"In the beginning was the Word, and the Word was with God, and the Word was God. The same was in the beginning with God. All things were made by*

*him; and without him was not any thing made that was made. In him was life; and the life was the light of men. And the light shineth in darkness; and the darkness comprehended it not. There was a man sent from God, whose name was John. The same came for a witness, to bear witness of the Light, that all men through him might believe. He was not that Light, but was sent to bear witness of that Light. That was the true Light, which lighteth every man that cometh into the world." (KJV)*

It is clear the light discussed in the Bible is Jesus himself. The way he acted and reacted to people and circumstances is an ideal model for all of his believers to follow, especially in a fallen world full of darkness. Jesus came into the world and took on a body that was made of flesh and blood. In Hebrew Chapter 2:14.

*"Forasmuch then as the children are partakers of flesh and blood, he also himself likewise took part of the same; that through death he might destroy him that had the power of death, that is, the devil." (KJV)*

During Christ's walk on Earth, he did not let anyone's actions cause an adverse reaction to dim his light; neither did any of his actions cause him to dim his light. In essence, Jesus kept his light at 100. An analogy that is relatable to the current time, he maintained a light that was similar to a 100 Watt light bulb at all times. Jesus was an enlightened being full of God's wisdom, knowledge, understanding, patience, mercy, joy, and love. The challenge imposed on humankind is to be able to reflect his light into this dark and fallen world can be found in John 12:35-36:

*"Then Jesus said unto them, Yet a little while is the light with you. Walk while ye have the light, lest darkness come upon you: for he that walketh in darkness knoweth not whither he goeth. While ye have light, believe in the light, that ye may be the children of light. These things spake Jesus, and departed, and did hide himself from them." (KJV)*

It can be inferred that Jesus left and hid because he wanted everyone to exercise their free-will and choose if they're going to be a reflection of his light or the darkness. In essence, do you want to live a life that reflects Jesus where no one, but you can choose to dim your light through negative actions or reactions of others? God and Jesus are the source of any light that bears truth; when faced with dark forces, it is in your complete control to choose if you will let your light shine, or be dimmed.

What to take from this Chapter:

1. Love the person, not the sin.

2. All people living can obtain salvation through Christ, so forgive to be forgiven – Love, so that you can receive Love.

3. Put your faith in God, not fortune-tellers.

4. If you enjoy wicked things, wicked things will come. So please, change the channel.

5. God and Jesus are your sources of life and light

6. Only you can dim your light. Choose to be that reflective 100 Watt light in a world full of dark forces.

# Chapter 9 – Know Your Armor. Now Put It On!

Life is full of tests, trials, temptations, and tribulations. To be more specific:

1. Test your strength and faith;

2. Try your acts and reactions;

3. Tempt your desires and self-control; and

4. Tribulations to reveal your endurance for victory or defeat.

As you live on this earth there will be some good days and some bad days, Matthew 4:45 states:

> *"That ye may be the children of your Father which is in heaven: for he maketh his sun to rise on the evil and on the good, and sendeth rain on the just and on the unjust." (KJV)*

The self-examining question we must ask ourselves is, "Are we prepared for the battles and conflicts that may arise?" The Apostle Paul provided some concise (short) guidance concerning the spiritual and mental armor Christians should wear at all times, Ephesians 6:10–18:

*"Finally, be strong in the Lord and in his mighty power. Put on the full armor of God, so that you can take your stand against the devil's schemes. For our struggle is not against flesh and blood, but against the rulers, against the authorities, against the powers of this dark world and against the spiritual forces of evil in the heavenly realms. Therefore put on the full armor of God, so that when the day of evil comes, you may be able to stand your ground, and after you have done everything, to stand. Stand firm then, with the belt of truth buckled around your waist, with the breastplate of righteousness in place, and with your feet fitted with the readiness that comes from the gospel of peace. In addition to all this, take up the shield of faith, with which you can extinguish all the flaming arrows of the evil one. Take the helmet of salvation and the sword of the Spirit, which is the word of God. And pray in the Spirit on all occasions with all kinds of prayers and requests. With this in mind, be alert and always keep on praying for all the Lord's people." (KJV)*

**The Belt of Truth** – Serves as assurance and security; knowing the truth keeps you from following false delusions that lead to chaos (confusion). Always remain firm and secure in the truth because the world is full of deceit. Standing in truth means you stand with God, who is and will always be Truth.

**Breastplate of Righteousness** – Breastplates are known to protect vital organs (heart, lungs, liver, stomach) from close and far encounters. To have a breastplate of righteousness means you know right from wrong, but will always choose to live right. By living righteously builds integrity (reliable/honest) which in turn creates a strong breastplate of armor. The opposite would be wicked/weak armor that is not strong, cannot endure, and is decrepit. Just keep in mind, wickedness can be pierced by other wicked things and most certainly things that are righteous.

**Feet fitted with the readiness that comes from the Gospel of Peace** – Feet are designed to help with swift mobility and good traction. To have your feet fitted with readiness to spread the Gospel (Good News) of peace, you want to have the traction for swift and stable movement. Your movement should always be seeking peace and spreading the news concerning the salvation provided by Christ with the promise of eternal life.

***Shield of Faith*** – A shield serves as a second layer of protection that can take a blow thrown by an enemy close, or at a distance. If your faith in God is strong, you know that nothing can harm you *(Isaiah 54:17 – No weapon that is formed against thee shall prosper)*. However, that is not to say you will not have some test, trials, temptations, and tribulations in your lifetime. While you endure the slings and arrows of life, you must strive to a live a life that emulates Christ and recruits others like a true disciple. So be prepared to put your Faith to work, because *"Faith without works is dead." (James 2:17 KJV)*

***Helmet of Salvation*** – Designed to protect the mind and thoughts from wicked schemes, false teachings, and tricks. To put the helmet of salvation on, you have the full knowledge that no matter what happens that Christ came to redeem humankind from their sins. Hence, you will have eternal life by remaining a believer and worker of Christ.

***Sword of the Spirit*** – The word of God is truthful and sharp; having knowledge of His word and promise makes you a force to be reckoned with. A Sword is a two-edged sword that can cut your friend, foe, and even yourself. Knowing you have an instrument that demands respect, you will yield to it for direction, correction, and perfection.

There seems to be a great deal of Armor that protects the front of your body, while your back remains exposed. The truth of the matter, God has given you the gift of life so that you can move forward through life. As for your exposed back, it is and never will be vulnerable (weak), because God got your back!!! (Along with your front, side, top, and bottom.)

*Isaiah 58:8 - Then your light will break forth like the dawn, and your healing will quickly appear; then your righteousness will go before you, and the glory of the Lord will be your rear guard (NIV).*

Things to take from this chapter:

1. Put on the armor of God every day

2. God has your back.

Reference: https://lifehopeandtruth.com

# Chapter 10 – The Art and Science of Forgiveness

*"Woe unto the world because of offences! For it must needs be that offences come; but woe to that man by whom the offence cometh" (Matthew 18:7 KJV)*

To begin to understand forgiveness you have to understand the impact of the offense caused by an offender. Any offense can be broken down into multiple categories and levels; however, this book will only address two overarching types of offences: Un-intentional and Intentional.

Un-intentional is an offense which the offending person did not mean to cause injury or damage either: physically, mentally, socially, financially, or spiritually. An example of an unintentional offense is a car accident that can cause bodily injury including death. The impact can be minor or severe; from a scratch to your car or death of someone close to you.

The art of forgiveness starts with preparation of your mind and having an understanding that offenses (small and large) are going to happen, either caused by others or yourself. Having the foreknowledge (know the future) that life and the people who share space and time with you are going to cross paths at some point in time. Some encounters friendly and others not so pleasant. The science behind forgiveness starts with knowing that you want to be forgiven for an offense (damage or injury) you may cause. It is essential to know that God has forgiven you of your sins; in turn, you are expected to exercise the same for those who offend you.

Although un-intentional offenses are easier to forgive than intentional offenses, the art and science behind forgiveness remain the same. Intentional offenses are at a higher level because the offender planned and wanted to cause injury and damage. Being a victim or offender concerning an intentional offense is difficult because it deeply addresses matters of the heart and mind of both parties. The act behind any offense can cause transferring feelings and emotions; which the offender's aggressive actions can transfer negative emotions and feelings to a victim that can last a lifetime. In preparation of any offense, a suspecting victim must be practicing the art of forgiveness by being mindful of offenses that may come and responding appropriately. The art of practicing forgiveness is difficult for any victim. However, the science of forgiveness must exist so that you don't become a prisoner of negative thoughts, resentment, and retaliation. By being a prisoner under negative thoughts consumes your being and changes your heart, focus, and drive.

Plenty of people would say, "Easier said than done…" Well, to respond to that pessimistic (negative) point of view, No one ever said it would be easy. That is why it is an "Art" to prepare your mind to exercise forgiveness and a "Science" implementing forgiveness after an offense occurs. By having a heart and mind ready to forgive creates a light of knowledge and path of wisdom; this leads to forgiveness and a rapid recovery no matter if the offense was unintentional or intentional.

Another perspective when it comes to offenses, do your best to take your focus off being the victim of an offense and place it on God who has already forgiven you for your trespasses. We are all humans and according to Romans 3:23:

*"For all have sinned, and come short of the glory of God" (KJV)*

As an offender, when you sin against God and man, acknowledging (admitting) your mistake is the beginning of the process of receiving forgiveness. Being in a state of denial of any offense is not a healthy or intelligent choice because of the expression "Woe." As discussed in Chapter 7, "Woe" is a state of hell that expands across various negative dimensions; such as, misery, affliction, trouble, and despair that will block your dreams, goals, and aspirations. Everything you think could go wrong will go wrong in your life, if you remain in a state of denial. The more a person goes into denial they lose sight of reality and don't recall the negative seeds they planted when they offended others. Eventually, the negative seeds will grow, and the only person that can truly consume the fruits thereof is the person who planted the seeds in the first place. The person living in denial will have a future full of trouble and would ignorantly question, "Why are bad things always happening to me?"

Once you can accept your wrong and apologize to both God and the victim you are putting the science of forgiveness in action. Therefore, you place yourself on a path of gaining God's favor. Matthew 5:23-24:

> *"Therefore if thou bring thy gift before the alter, and there rememberest that thy brother hath ought against thee; Leave there thy gift before the alter, and go thy way; first be reconciled to thy brother, and then come and offer thy gift."* (KJV)

The vital aspect of what is being conveyed is to recall that you needed forgiveness for something; therefore, have a heart and mind ready to forgive when an offense crosses your path. I like to refer to it as, "The art and science of reciprocity."

The mere idea of not forgiving an offense makes you a prisoner to the offense. By inadvertent (accidental) default, you may be in danger of giving up your right of reciprocity (tradeoff) provided by the Blood of Jesus; because you are sinking in the sin of un-forgiveness. Matthew 18:15-18:

> *"Moreover if thy brother shall trespass against thee, go and tell him his fault between thee and him alone: if he shall hear thee, thou hast gained thy brother. But if he will not hear thee, then take with thee one or two more, that in the mouth of two or three witnesses every word may be established. And if he shall neglect to hear them, tell it unto the church: but if he neglect to hear the church, let him be unto thee as an heathen man and a publican. Verily I say unto you,*

*whatsoever ye shall bind on earth shall be bound in heaven: and whatsoever ye shall loose on earth shall be loosed in heaven." (KJV)*

To be an un-repented offender or unforgiving victim will eventually follow you to your judgment. On the other hand, being a repented offender and forgiving victim will free you from any offense.

The main points of this chapter:

1. The "Art" of forgiveness is about preparing your "Heart" to forgive.

2. The Science of forgiveness is the application of forgiving (Either Offender or Victim).

3. Be mindful that you have received forgiveness of your sins; therefore, provide the same courtesy to those who offend you.

4. Un-forgiveness is a prison that can give you feelings aligned with misery and hell.

# Chapter 11 – Parent and Child Fellowship

This chapter caters to parents and those wanting to be parents that set the pace and tone concerning a positive relationship with your child, children, or future offspring, but written for young adults. The content can be experienced with children to bring about a better understanding of both parties, now and in the future. Remember it is your time to spend with one another.

To reiterate, God is about decency and order. If someone steps out of order, it serves no purpose to do the same; it only leads to a chaotic society. For instance, if your earthly father should do something that is out of order and not favorable in the sight of God, it must not sway you from respecting him and remaining orderly yourself. Ultimately, God will hold anyone in your charge accountable for every wrong or right thing accomplished. It is your job to maintain order and respect your elders, with readiness to teach those younger than you.

You were born, when you were born. God planned it that way and put it into His order. If He wanted you here before your elders, He would have made it that way. However, your situation is your situation good or bad. To elevate yourself you must remain orderly even in a fallen and corrupt world. God seeks a person like Abraham who will make a strong foundation by obeying Him. Stand erect (straight) like an antenna, ready to receive His many blessings in a turbulent world.

When sitting down and reflecting on my childhood, I think of how my father a well-respected Deacon in our community, always worked hard to provide for me. I am truly thankful…. Through him, I was able to grasp how my relationship with my earthly father who I could see; should replicate the relationship I have with my Heavenly Father, who I don't see.

My Father was and is a good representation of God, meaning he made every attempt to do things that were Godly in my presence, in hopes of things rubbing off on me. For example, I cannot recall ever hearing my father swear or curse. He was slow to anger and never beat me down mentally or physically when I made a mistake. If anything he was reserved and quiet, but when he spoke you knew he meant what he was saying (It cut right to the matter at hand).

Overall, there are many things a parent can do to ensure the fellowship with their child does not break their bond:

1. Examine your own life and be a positive example to your child.

2. Communicate with the younger generations about your childhood and lessons learned.

3. Make it a habit of spending 15 to 30 minutes with them each day.

4. Take your child to a Bible teaching church.

5. Pray with your children and teach them that conversation with God is like conversing with you (take turns praying).

6. Read your Bible or a Children's Bible.

At an early age, a child likes to imitate the first adult role model they see. They like to be around their parents and older siblings. They enjoy helping, fixing, and preparing things, anything to receive the approval of the older generation. Many parents miss an opportunity to help shape and mold their vibrant children to be a young adult that will always respect and appreciate Dad or Mom. Usually, most parents send their children away out of fear of them getting in the way or hurt. That is the protective nature of a parent; however, there are things one can do to include your offspring without completely disinteresting them from grown-up activities. One way is by giving them a tool/device and let them stand nearby to watch you. Then, when it is safe, have the child hand you the tool and compliment him/her on a job well done. Yeah, some jobs are too dangerous for a young child to be around but do what you can to include them. What may seem like a minor task to you can be a significant task to them, especially when you give them that pat on the back, "Way to go… job well done!"

As your child grows older (into adolescence) they will seek their own identity and style. Most likely they will spend more time with their friends to talk about the opposite sex and other interests. Becoming older is also a crucial time in their life, but if you are involved in the early part of a child's life and a role model, they will never forget the things you shared. If anything, the child will use what they witnessed in you as his/her foundation for when they get older and have children of their own.

It is essential that children have their space and your trust, but not too much because you are a parent. Explain drugs and alcohol on a regular basis and let them know the pitfalls for indulging in such activities. Make your child aware of the things they could lose in life because of engaging and investing in something that does nothing to increase their existence but only steals from them (like health, mental state, relationships, and money).

Young adulthood is an excellent time to start engaging in conversations about what you experienced when you were their age, be honest and truthful. Focus on your successes and mistakes as it will build honesty between the two of you. And when a child makes a mistake, do not react negatively. Always be prepared to respond the following day; silence upon receiving bad news is usually excellent discipline for any child.

The only time a child must receive immediate discipline is when you know he or she did something intentional to hurt someone else. As for simple mistakes, be reserved in discussing and executing any punishment. Silence alone can help keep a child in check and leaving them guessing on what you are thinking, which will lead a child to chastise (punish) their self mentally.

Do your best to attend church often and expose them to a preacher who teaches from the Bible. Doing so gives your child a chance to build their knowledge and to come into his/her understanding of what God expects of them. To support his/her spiritual development, understand that a human's average attention span is about twenty-five (25) minutes. Therefore, finding a church where the preacher is knowledgeable and brief (short) is advantageous to any child's spiritual development.

When home alone, pray with your offspring one on one, or in a family setting. I recall my father having family prayer every Sunday morning before going to church. Things like that stick with you well into adulthood. An excellent place to start is the Lord's Prayer and most important discuss with them what it means (Matthew 6:5-13 KJV):

> *"And when thou prayest, thou shalt not be as the hypocrites are: for they love to pray standing in the synagogues and in the corners of the streets, that they may be seen of men. Verily I say unto you; they have their reward. But thou, when you prayest, enter into thy closet, and when thou hast shut the door, pray to thy Father which is in secret, and thy Father which seeth in secret shall reward thee openly. But when ye pray, use not vain repetitions, as the heathen do: for they think they shall be heard for their much speaking. Be not ye therefore like unto them: for your Father knoweth what things ye have need of, before ye ask him. After this manner therefore pray ye:"*

*Our Father which are in heaven* (Think of God who is in heaven and owns it forever)

*Hallowed be thy name* (To set His name as Holy and respect His name – remember the third commandment and how it ties back in).

*Thy Kingdom Come* (Know and believe that God's kingdom will be coming to this earth and will not fail).

*Thy will be done on earth* (Know that God's will supersedes your desires, wants, and needs. Submit to His will and things that edify Him, not yourself).

*As it is in heaven* (His will is taking place in heaven as we speak, and is being delivered down to the earth through our willing participation and exercising our free will to serve Him).

*Give us this day our daily bread* (God will meet your needs. And possibly your wants if it does not disrupt His will).

*And forgive us our debts* (Ask God for forgiveness and avoid repeating your mistakes).

*As we forgive our debtors* (Be willing and ready to forgive those who offend you or steal from you. Especially when we all need forgiveness from God. Exercise forgiveness because that's what you would want from the Lord). Matthew 6:14 & 15

*And lead us not into temptation* (Keep the things we lust after away from us or those things that cause us to violate God's commandments).

*But deliver us from evil* (When evil comes, which it will; remove us from it. Just like when tempted, God does provide a way out to allow you to flee from it like it was our worst nightmare. Scripture to support this is 1 Corinthians 10:13:

*"There hath no temptation taken but such as is common to man: but God is faithful, who will not suffer you to be tempted above that ye are able; but will with the temptation also make a way to escape, that ye may be able to bear it."*

*For thine is the kingdom* (The Kingdom belongs to God and a reward to those who walk in His Son's ways.)

*And the Power* (God can act effectively with no resistance)

*And the Glory* (God has the praise and recognition that is more than deserved).

*Forever* (God and all He has is continuous and never-ending).

The above is something significant left by Christ for all of us to follow as a guide toward communicating with our heavenly Father. The thing that gets me is the secret part, which seems to be the key, not doing it for a show, but praying in one's closet to build that personal relationship with God.

Also, when praying, emphasize the importance of praying for others before one's self. Treat your prayers like a conversation with God. Come up with an order on different types of prayers. An excellent order for praying can be memorized using the acronym A.C.T.S. which stands for, Adoration, Confession, Thanksgiving, & Supplication. Start with appreciation (adoration) of God, Son, and Holy Ghost. Confess your sins and where you have fallen short. Be thankful for the time and family members. Ask (supplication) for the blessing of those in need (spiritual, health, mental, social, and financial), nation's leaders, those seeking the Lord and those who are lost.

When you have an order when praying to God, the prayers are much easier to communicate. Just like when you want to ask your earthly father something, there is a way you greet him before asking for what you need.

Another thing you can do to help build your relationship is to read the Bible with your offspring (children). If you are not sure about what you are reading, acquire a Bible Dictionary or Commentary. Such books are helpful references to aid in explaining the Bible. Solomon wrote certain books in the Bible, (Proverbs, Song of Solomon, and Ecclesiastic) that hold a great deal of wisdom, especially as it pertains to family relationships and life in general.

In your relationship with your child, do your best never to lose sight that you are their parent and able to provide for him/her through God's blessings. Be a friend to your child, but it is more critical for you to be their parent. After all, your child will come across many friends, yet only one set of earthly parents and one heavenly Father.

In your attempt to be that parent/friend it may seem like a difficult task to say no or set specific examples, but to give you a broader perspective; an earthly child and Heavenly Father are watching an earthly parent. It's kind of a pinch effect where God (the Ultimate Superior) and a child, (a subordinate) are evaluating you on how you live your life, and treat others.

Yes, sons and daughters have the commandment to honor fathers and mothers. But it is vital that one practices an upright life that deserves honor from God. So, when you make a mistake or commit a sin; you expect God to give you mercy, kindness, and forgiveness. The other side, be prepared to do the same for your child if they make a mistake.

*"And, ye Fathers, provoke not your children to wrath: but bring them up in the nurture and admonition of the Lord."* (Ephesians 6:4 KJV)

*"Fathers, provoke not your children to anger, lest they be discouraged."* (Colossians 3:21 KJV)

Based on these two verses, it is clear that mentally beating our children over a mistake does nothing but provokes (stirs) them to anger and discourages them in so many ways. When it comes time to disciplining a child: be slow to react, be concise in your words, and just in your punishment.

The Old Testament can be summarized as a time when people came to God, then strayed (drift away) from God. Mainly in the books of Kings and Chronicles, you hear of Kings of Judah and Israel who have done two things: Good in the eyes of the Lord or Evil in the eyes of the

Lord. The kings who did good in the eyes of the Lord were compliant with God's commandments, while those who did evil worshipped idol gods. With a great deal of change between good and evil kings mostly by inherent right, one can see an apparent disconnect in parenting/mentoring. Disconnects occurred when a royal child did not understand his roots or the relationship God established with His people, which caused him to stray from God's way. Therefore, one can deduce (gather) that not being involved in a child's life and failing to educate a child in God's way; can leave them to cleave to other ideologies or false teachings of those who may friend them. Parent and Child fellowship supports the need for a parent to be involved in a child's life and keep them from the pitfalls which God does not want us falling in. We must remind our children of God's love, kindness, longsuffering, and mercy.

In summary of this chapter, it is essential to:

1. Examine your own life according to God's laws. Be a living example to your child.

2. Take your child to church and teach them how to pray to God to build that personal relationship with the Almighty.

3. Control your reactions to a child's mistakes and practice this by anticipating their folly. If you're not sure, reflect on your childhood (mistakes made by you, friends, and siblings).

4. Silence is usually golden and stronger than a rod of discipline at times. Do not let your children forget God's goodness and mercy.

# Chapter 12 – Your Temple

What walks on four legs in the morning, two legs in the afternoon, and three legs in the evening? Give up? It's you, a Human. I always liked that riddle because it symbolizes (example) human's walk in life, but compressed into a symbolic day. The morning represents the time we crawl as a child on hands and knees. The afternoon represents when we walk on two feet during the mid-part of our lives. And the evening, the golden years when we walk with our two feet and a cane.

The physical characteristics of human development throughout life are self-evident. The stages from infancy to adulthood are something most of us have seen either through observing: ourselves, father, grandfathers, or children.

Below is a quick summary concerning human development that is referenced from various sources (Erik Erikson's Stages of Development, Child Development Institute, and Britannica):

1. Infants and Toddlers (1 to 3 years old) need constant attention and want their needs met instantly. During this stage in life, they only have a concept of themselves and exercise selfish tendencies.

2. Toddlers to Adolescents to Teenagers (4 to 19), experience realization of others and an increasing level of independence from parents. Especially during the adolescent stage, seeking one's own identity is the primary drive. One tries to find their identity through peers and feels the need to escape any parental identity. Also, the building of one's reputation and status among their peers is a significant drive.

3. Adulthood (20 and on) is the stage in which we wrestle with: intimacy, isolation, despair, stagnation, and caring for the upcoming generation.

Knowing what is going on inside your mind, especially at certain stages in your life is beneficial (good) towards your understanding of yourself as a parent or child, in light of the decisions one may or may not make. As young adults develop into adulthood and beyond, we have a responsibility to perfect ourselves: spiritually, mentally, physically, socially, and financially.

In addressing your temple, it is your physical body for which you have a responsibility to take care of; meaning eating right and exercising. You are responsible for the body your soul occupies; it is indeed a priceless gift from God.

So just like your favorite car, you put the right gas and oil in the car. Why not put the right foods and liquids in your body? There is a book about nutrition that expresses, *"You are what you eat...."* (Lindlahr published 1942) So, put the right things in your body without over-doing it or under-doing it....

If you take your car out for a drive and put its performance to the test, why not take your body out for a spin. For example, take part in some sporting event: basketball, soccer, bowling, jogging, weight lifting, swimming or activity that gets your heart pumping, lungs expanding, and blood flowing. Overall, go out and break a sweat once a week or every day. Indeed, you will feel great about yourself and more energized.

I can recall as a kid that playing: touch football, basketball, soccer, and baseball with my friends were some of the activities I looked forward to after school or on the weekends. Unfortunately, handheld and home video games came on the scene that cut down on our outside play time. It seemed these video games captured the attention of most of my friends who would prefer to stay in the house and play a sports video game with their fingers instead of going out and playing the sport with their entire body. The era of video games seems to have stolen plenty of things from America's children: creativity, activity, and ingenuity. Instead of truly realizing our potential, we were focused on bleeps of light on a handheld or TV screen. Electronic usage could be a good reason why other countries are catching up to America technologically speaking; because video games are diverting young Americans' attention.

As for the body's fuel, there are times when your body (flesh) will crave certain foods and drinks. Also, our body will prefer a certain level of relaxation and exercising is just another level of discomfort to support doing nothing. Another key to having a close relationship with God is for your mind to master your body, not your body mastering your mind. Mastering one's self is the main conflict within ourselves that we all wrestle.

So what some people do to get their body in check is, fast. Some fast by only drinking water or eating only at night. A good practice when fasting is to drink water throughout the day to force the body into submission and control it. The stomach growls, but at some point in time, it will stop when the mind tells it.

The same with any addiction, you always crave the things that are bad for you like alcohol or nicotine. The key to going cold turkey is willpower and not giving in to what your body wants. When you can refuse that extra piece of your favorite dessert or say no to any drug you think brings about pleasure, you have truly mastered your body.

To start your journey of mind over matter, win the internal battle within yourself. If you never tried drugs, take a stance now and say I have no need to experiment with drugs, nor do I want to contaminate my temple. By being faithful to your temple, you avoid the consequences of indulging in poor habits. However, remember you are no better than a person who has allowed their body to succumb to such contaminants. Jesus said in Mark 7:15:

> *"There is nothing from without a man that entering into him can defile him: but the things that which come out of him, those are they that defile the man."*
> *(KJV)*

The things that defile a man can be found in Mark 7:20-23 of the same chapter and reiterated in Chapter 6:

*"And he said, That which cometh out of the man, that defileth the man. For from within, out of the heart of men, proceed evil thoughts, adulteries, fornications, murders, thefts, covetousness, wickedness, deceit, lasciviousness, an evil eye, blasphemy, pride, foolishness: All these evil things come from within, and defile the man." (KJV)*

In essence, drugs and alcohol alone don't defile you, but the acts you may commit and the words you speak while under the influence (not of a sober mind) could defile you. That's why it is in your best interest to be in control of your free will. While at the same time, be a good steward (manager) by putting good things in the temple God gave you. Further, you have an obligation (duty) to be a living example and help those who may have fallen.

So your body/temple is a priceless piece of equipment designed by God for you to exercise free will over it, but with a conscious choice for you to control your free will that serves God's purpose. Eventually, your body is going to fail you one day. Your soul will depart from your body as it returns to the earth, and soon you will be given a new body. However, in the meantime, the mind/soul God has given you can either be close to God or separate from God. I don't know about you, but I prefer my soul to be close to God, my Father, and creator who is pure and loving. How about you?

In summary:

1. Take care of your body; it's the only one you have.

2. Put good things into your temple.

3. Be of a sober mind, free yourself of unnecessary contaminants.

4. Exercise - Do not let your "body" master your "mind," but let your "mind" master your "body."

# Chapter 13 – The Difference "Between" an Adult & a Child

There is a scripture that helps us to understand the mental transition (change) from childhood to adulthood, and it's found in, 1 Corinthians 13:11:

*"When I was a child, I spake as a child, I understood as a child, I thought as a child: but when I became a man, I put away childish things."(KJV)*

Indeed time has, or will develop you into an adult physically; it is something that is naturally inevitable (expected). However, the same does not apply to your mind and thoughts. When you step out on your own, ask yourself, "Will I or do I… have the mind of a child or of an Adult?" To be honest, the choice is up to you, and how you decide to exercise your free will and time.

Now, what is the difference between an adult and a child?

| The mind of an Adult | The mind of a Child |
|---|---|
| Takes responsibility for their actions and gives recognition to others. | Takes no responsibility for their actions and blames others. |
| Is aware of the consequences and risks. | Will do things without thinking about the consequences or risks. |
| Ability to put things in order (prioritize). | Creates disorder. |

| The mind of an Adult | The mind of a Child |
|---|---|
| Makes sacrifices and puts the comfort of others before their own. | Knows nothing about sacrifices and puts their own comfort before others, or no concern for others. |
| Doesn't make decisions that are spontaneous or based on emotions. | Makes spontaneous decisions that are often driven by emotion (Sets things in Disarray for others and themselves). |
| Is patient and understanding. | Impatient and lacks understanding. Seeks immediate gratification. |
| Humble and meek. | Boastful and aggressive. |
| A protector of others by providing security at multiple levels (Spiritual, Physical, Mental, Social, Financial). | Selfish and concerned with their own security. |
| Generous with time and resources. | Greedy with their time and resources. |
| Means what they say and says what they mean. (Word is their bond - Reliable). | Does not know the meaning of, "Your word is your bond," and has no problems making empty promises. (Unreliable) |
| Their mind controls fleshly cravings (Controls desires of promiscuous sex, excessive consumption of alcohol, or completely rejects substances like illegal drugs). | Their mind has no control over their fleshly cravings (Engages in promiscuous sex, excessive consumption of alcohol, or indulges in illegal drugs). |
| Flexible and willing to meet others half-way (compromise). | Stubborn and lacks understanding of the word "compromise." |
| Seeks peace over conflict; slow to anger and quick to reconcile. | Seeks conflicts instead of peace; quick to anger and avoids reconciliation. |

| The mind of an Adult | The mind of a Child |
|---|---|
| An adult is independent and strives to be independent with realistic long and short-term goals that have reasonable steps. | Is dependent on others with no plans for being independent themselves. |
| Always ready to give and seeks little to nothing in return. | Always ready to receive and gives little in return. |
| Ruled by faith, instead of fear. | Ruled by fear, instead of faith. |
| Has a driven mind for success. | Concerned with what they are driving (car), not how to be driven toward success. |
| Sympathetic and empathetic when others are suffering and in misery. | Takes pleasure in others who are suffering and in misery. |
| Can "Identify" characteristics and situations without "Judging" (does not give punishment or reward/non-prejudice/objective) | "Judges" characteristics and situations without "Identifying" (jumps to conclusions/lacks sufficient relevant facts/subjective) |
| Is aware of who lives within (Jesus). | Concerned with where and what they live in (house), not with who lives within them. |

Some adults are considered "adults" by law because of their age. However, their minds are still that of a child. It is funny how most young people want "respect" once they turn 18, but don't realize that respect is something you earn through your deeds and the steps you take toward your goals. The mentality of wanting respect without doing anything to deserve it falls under, Seeks immediate gratification.

The following are examples of adults who think like children are: fathers who put their own needs above their child. Or, the adult who buys a nice suit, before paying his rent or others he may owe.

On the flip side, some young adults under age 18 have a mind like an adult. For example, they work hard in school and hold jobs after school. They financially contribute to their family household or help out their parents by watching their younger siblings. Also, they have limited to no disciplinary problems in school and are aware of why they are in school.

Many other examples could support "A mind of an adult" and "A mind of a child" that is not mentioned in this book. Nevertheless, the choice to be an adult physically is in the hands of nature, but to have a mind like an adult is a conscious choice it's not automatic or natural.

What to take from this Chapter:

Choose your mind; Adult or Child?

# Chapter 14 – Taboo of Idleness

Idleness is being useless, inactive, and lazy. To reiterate from Chapter five, it is a waste of the gift God has given you, life and time. To live is to be alive, and to be alive, you should engage in activities that edify God and enhance your future. Proverbs 19:15:

*"Slothfulness casteth into a deep sleep; and an idle soul shall suffer hunger."* *(KJV)*

The same way we feed ourselves food and liquids, we must also feed our souls with good things that increase our awareness of God, the earth, and humankind. The food for our soul is: connecting with God, seeking knowledge, being of service to others (To exercise this is truly feeding your soul).

To reiterate (repeat), sitting around constantly watching TV is similar to being dead, where you are watching others. Now is this totally a bad thing? Yes, when you constantly watch TV. You can view some programs to get some form of a perspective or understanding of what others may be experiencing. However, the continuous watching of TV robs you of life. I know some people who are obsessed with watching the news, which the majority of information is bad news about the world and what is going on in other people's lives. They can sit in front of the TV from sun up to sun down, consumed with the problems of the world, but do nothing to get out into the world to change something or make a difference in someone's life.

Further, there is idle talk when you say things that go nowhere. Growing up, I used to have an acquaintance (occasional friend) who always claimed that he was bored, but had no idea of what to do to cure his boredom. If you suggested any activity that involved physical involvement he would turn that idea down in a minute. If you asked, what he would like to do, he still would not have a clue or a plan. He would sit around and complain, which is a form of idle talk. Proverbs 14:23:

> "In all labour there is profit: but the talk of the lips tendeth only to penury (poverty)." (KJV)

The significant aspect of this verse is that having something to do is beneficial (good), and that talk is cheap and a prelude to poverty. So it is essential to look for something to do and speak positive things into existence. Yeah, we may exhibit some frustrations in life, but stay busy with minimal complaints and maximum compliments. One thing I learned is that people, regardless of their nature, always seek the knowledge and companionship of someone who is productive and positive in life. People even if they despise the person for being so driven and positive will still seek their counsel to get a perspective that may be hard for them to grasp on their own; especially because their world may be steeped (soaked) in negative thoughts and problems.

Another aspect of idle talk is the use of profanity or harsh language. The practice of cursing and using any explicit (curse) as a noun, verb, adjective, or pronoun builds nothing. This style of communication can only tear down others and leaves a negative impression. In essence, a person who curses a lot is a person with a limited vocabulary. Further, Ephesians 4:29:

> "Let no corrupt communication proceed out of your mouth, but that which is good to the use of edifying, that it may minister grace unto the hearers."(KJV)

The practice of speaking good things will only breed good things, especially if the words you speak inspire your listeners. Maya Angelou said, *"People will forget what you said, people will forget what you did, but people will never forget how you made them feel."*

In an Electrical Engineering course, I learned that the positive end of a battery gains and the negative end loses. If I was asked to choose what end of the battery of life I would want to be on, it is the positive end, where I'm constantly gaining.

Now, what are some things that you can do to fight off idleness and idle talk? Have a plan to do positive things. Ask yourself what you can do to increase your relationship with God, knowledge, or help someone?

For better clarification, have a plan to read whenever boredom sneaks into your mind, read something that will energize you. A good thing to read is the number one seller: The Bible. The best way to get to know the Lord is to understand what He says and how He inspired others. Most Christians profess that they want to get to know Jesus better; all anyone has to do is read the writing in red and understand the words that He spoke. The entire Bible is a road map to glory and instant cure for boredom, especially to an hungered soul that wants to be full.

Also, there are self-help books to increase your knowledge of the world. Vocabulary books to expand your diction, Latin and Greek books to increase your knowledge concerning the origins of words. Plus, there are grammar and punctuation books to improve your understanding of written communication, and word problem books to help enhance your comprehension and math skills.

If there is something you always wanted to know about or don't understand, purchase a book on the topic and read about it. Also, consult with someone who may be knowledgeable of a topic, career, or subject. It may be easier than what you initially thought.

Further, having a plan of service to help those in need is another approach. For example, there are senior citizen centers that would love for you to volunteer your services. By the way, here's a little secret, senior citizens are a wealth of information and wisdom that are waiting for a young ear to be filled and soul to be fed. Plenty of life's lessons could be learned and mistakes avoided, if only the youth had the time and patience to sit and listen to a senior citizen. A senior citizen most likely witnessed or experienced the same problems that plague all of humankind through all generations.

On the flip side, help a child that is younger than you, be a friend to someone who has a disability. There are so many ways you can fill your soul with knowledge while at the same time, fill someone else's life with joy.

The big picture; life is a big circle. At one point in your life, you were a child growing up and in need of someone to encourage you. On the other side of the circle, you are getting older and going to want someone to talk to you about the things you experienced in life.

To be idle does no one any good. Whenever you feel like you're bored or being lazy, think of a statue that is sitting in the middle of a park. Then ask yourself, do I want to be a statue? The answer is probably, No. Even the idea of constantly standing on a street corner with friends talking about rumors or something that happened in the past is considered being idle. On the flip side, the things that are more memorable are the times when you accomplish positive things with a group like sports or projects.

As for resting it is different because it is something you do after working and implementing your plans. The goal is to re-energize your being, just like sleep for the body. Your body falls asleep for approximately one-third of your life to re-energize. Even if you are sitting around doing nothing, your body such as; your heart, lungs, brain, blood, and other major and minor organs remain at work for the benefit of your body's survival. Therefore, your body is entitled to rest, even though your mind may or may not be idle (involuntary activity and dreaming).

Overall, activities like playing sports and reading can enhance your being by increasing your health and knowledge. A good analogy I heard in health class is that between the ages of 1 to 100 your body symbolizes a powerful race car to a cruising Rolls Royce. When you don't take the car out of the garage to test drive or show its power, speed, or elegance the vehicle becomes obsolete. So why do the same thing to your mind and body?

The difference between rest and being idle is rest means you take a break from work to re-energize, with intentions of accomplishing more work after a rest. To be idle is doing nothing with plans of accomplishing nothing.

God encourages rest, but not idleness.

In summary, the points to extract from this chapter:

1. Idleness is like being a statue in a park.

2. Have a plan to cure an idle life and talk.

3. Be ready to read (Bible) when the idle monster tries to creep in your mind.

4. Be ready to serve others when the idle monster appears.

5. Know the difference between rest and idleness.

102

# Chapter 15 – Life is No Music Video

Just imagine, its morning and you wake up, jump out of your bed, take a shower, then get dressed in the nicest gear (clothes) money could buy. You slip on the latest limited edition kicks (sneakers) or expensive shoes. You head out your front door and Bam!!! Loud music starts playing, and on your front lawn, three dozen nice looking people choreograph dancing on your mother's flower bed and around your Brand New Bentley and Mercedes Benz. You smile as they dance towards you and nod your head to the music. Your friends are coming up to show you some love. They have diamonds and gold all around their necks, all provided by you, the star, the man/woman.

OK… WAKE UP NOW!!!

If you haven't noticed, that really does not happen in real life. Yeah, the images you see in music videos exist, but it's not real. The performers are screened, clothing picked, and dance moves rehearsed. All the mundane things are provided by marketers to keep you drooling and at the same time, focusing on things insignificant and contrary (against) to God's plan for your life.

The true and sad part about these images that are depicted on TV is the fact that the entertainers portraying these lifestyles in videos do not have this going on in their real lives. If anyone was to drive past the home of a musical celebrity, I'm quite sure they would not see what takes place in their videos taking place on their property.

Yeah, you can go to a nightclub where celebrities are catered to and praised but, you have to ask, "Is what I see on TV, really taking place?"

Do you or will you experience the level of enjoyment that they are portraying in their videos? Doubtful…! If anything, most people at these events are quite envious (despises) of the entertainer's success, unless they are invited into the VIP section to meet the celebrity.

The critical thing to remember about what you see in a video is that it's not real life and far from it. It seems as though every music video depicts the same images. You have an entertainer doing his piece in different clothes, with different fictitious (make believe) backgrounds, and handsome people dancing around them. They all have nice cars and jewelry. Also, some videos are boastful (remember the earlier chapter), while at the same time demeaning and disparaging to women. It would be shocking if one of them broke away from the norm.

Nonetheless, the point is not to bite the hype the media is trying to push in front of you; doing so would consist of measuring success by achieving worldly wealth, as well as, practicing promiscuous sex whenever possible. What concerns me is the fact that most young people aspire to be a big-time rock or rap star, ball player, clothing designer, or entertainer. However, no one aspires to invent something to serve humankind better (For instance, developing the next best cell phone, discovering a new way to treat cancer, or changing laws that benefit all of society).

Is it wrong to dream of stardom…? Nah. However, is it wrong if it only edifies you only, without looking to be of service to others?

Indeed, God created you so that you can imagine and have dreams. Is it wrong to have stardom as your only plan? Well, if it is your single plan without having a backup plan, then "yes" it is wrong.

I strongly agree that wealth comes from the Lord… and from evil forces as well (to counter God's plan in this world for those who are lost). Regardless, one has to be vigilant (aware) and strong-minded about knowing where some sources of wealth come from, either God or from the evil forces.

Yes, it is a blessing to have a beautiful house, car, job, status, love, and appreciation from family and friends. Point being, let God and the wisdom He gives you be your guide toward these things. Having materialistic things are cool, but remember human nature; once you own something you have always desired, you tend to get bored with it very quickly.

The true measurement of success is measured by the number of people you help in this lifetime, not by one's wallet or toys. To measure success by one's wallet is foolish and shallow because you measure something of this earth, which no human can take to glory. However, the number of people you assisted on earth for the benefit of God's Kingdom is something that surpasses this world.

What to ascertain from this chapter is:

1. Don't fall for the false images and ideas presented by TV and Radio.

2. There are other careers greater than entertainment.

3. Don't measure success by the size of one's wallet or purse.

4. Strive for the riches of Heaven through good deeds, rather than obtain the wealth of this world by sinful means.

# Chapter 16 – Can't is a Curse Word

Can't is a curse word. Many people speak it with their mouth and throw it in front of their future without thinking. Saying "Can't" is convincing one's self of being unable to do something, which is usually driven by fear. However, God did not place humans on this earth to live in fear. He placed humans on this earth to have fellowship with Him, faith in his word, and dominion over all things.

If a person's mental perspective is negative and embracing "can't," their accomplishments will be few, if not any. A person's future success depends on a positive attitude, which can lead to positive things in life. While there may be bad days and moments that may get you down; the thing to remember is actions and reactions should always be positive. If negative, you should be reserved (silent).

As expressed in Chapter 10, do your best to anticipate problems that may occur, and to have planned reactions to avoid the negative things that lead to the "can't" monster. It is a good practice in avoiding problems and mitigating (reducing) the damage of unavoidable (going to happen) setbacks to stay positive for the sake of your present and future.

Another aspect is making sure you surround yourself with positive people. Individuals who sit around having pity parties should be acquaintances (associates) with limited contact unless they are seeking positive insight. Otherwise, their degree of negativity can be contagious (spread), and you can easily find yourself complaining about the same problems rather than finding solutions.

The purpose of being in school is to learn, removing yourself from the vicinity (location) of those who cause distractions is a good move. They're the negative forces that will hinder anyone's learning that can turn "can't" into a reality. For instance, while in class you should separate yourself from those who are not there for knowledge. Choosing not to move from the negative people when and if they act out can make one fortuitously (accidentally) guilty by association.

A shocking reality, but the sad truth is that jobs are more cliquish than high schools, where nepotism (favoring relatives) and cronyism (favoring friends) run rampant (widespread). The office favorites are promoted faster with a large margin of error, with a protection society that reduces or dismisses any errors. However, whenever someone is promoted (either justified or not); make it a habit of remaining positive by congratulating those who go up the corporate ladder. The kindness you demonstrate today could work in your favor tomorrow. Avoid the negative persona of that "can't or won't" be me. Instead, reverse the thinking into it "can or will" be me. In essence, the people you encourage today can be your support for future promotions or starting your own business for tomorrow.

Now, that does not mean you should lay down for issues that are not right, or absurd (ridiculous). You should stand for righteousness, and God's word no matter the circumstances for promotion comes from the Lord (Psalms 75:6-7)

> *"For promotion cometh neither from the east, nor from the west, nor from the south. But God is the judge: he putteth down one, and setteth up another." (KJV)*

The main things to extract from this chapter:

1. Remove "Can't" out of your vocabulary.

2. Be positive. When life is throwing lemons; prepare to make lemonade (multiple unknown authors).

3. Stay away from negative people and groups.

4. Decrease Complaints, Increase Compliments.

5. Choose the right battles.

# Chapter 17 – School

You have heard it time and time again, "Get an education!" You probably heard that education is the key to success, which is 100% correct. Education is the key to obtaining success and a more comfortable lifestyle. In essence, do what you legally and morally can to obtain an education (scholarships), even going into debt (student loans). The dividends (bonuses) by getting your Degree or Certification are far greater than if you don't pursue higher learning.

Yes… some people have become successful with limited education, but the chance of obtaining success is lower than those who seek higher learning. Meaning, you increase your chances of a comfortable lifestyle by getting an education as opposed to those who don't.

Now education is not just confined to obtaining a piece of paper, such as; a High School Diploma, College Degrees (undergraduate or graduate), or Certifications. Having the piece of paper demonstrates (shows) to employers and your future customers that you can receive, implement, and complete assignments. In short, it symbolizes your ability to finish what you started.

However, if you don't obtain that piece of paper, it's about taking the knowledge from the institution and applying what you learned to work for your benefit (regardless, it is still beneficial (good) to receive that piece of paper). Once again, it demonstrates to yourself and the world that you can meet and exceed requirements to solidify your abilities, capabilities, and credentials.

Now when you hear, "Get an education!" Be prepared to outline your goals and how you are going to let education work for you. Have goals - high goals.

Many people obtain an education in hopes of living a wealthy and luxurious life. Only a few set out to do what they like for self-fulfillment; others fall into careers they despise then wonder how they got there (?).

The primary goal of all people who pursue an education is to obtain independence, either from someone else's way of doing things or minimizing your chances of making a mistake. Strategically place yourself in a position of knowledge to bring about change. Look to own a business, for example, if you want to be a Doctor; set goals to have a practice, clinic, or hospital. If you strive to be an Attorney; look to own a Law Firm, become a judge or political leader. If you are looking to be a journalist; own a newspaper, magazine, radio, or television news station. If you are looking to become an electrician; own a contracting firm or supply store.

Learn what you can so that your knowledge becomes in demand. Know as much as you can to be self-sufficient. People will seek you to solve their problems at a cost determined by yourself, as an expert in your field.

There may be a point in your life when you obtain your education (degree, certification, or diploma) and need to work for someone else to apply and sharpen your skills; it is perfectly understandable and necessary. All of us require some form of mentorship, before being mentors ourselves. So yes, get the experience by working with someone who is established, learn from them, their successes and failures. However, never lose sight of branching out on your own.

The key to tackling education or any course is an attitude. Your attitude must have three points like the tip of an arrow. The main point is "your attitude," and it must be positive. The secondary points "obtain knowledge" and "apply what you learned."

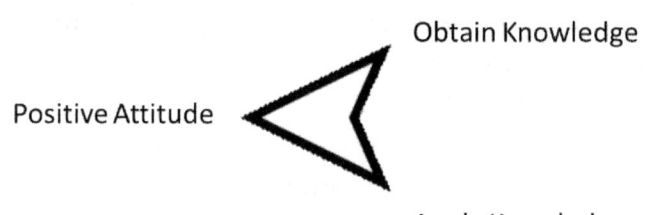

Many would question, why knowledge isn't the main point? Well, if you don't have a positive attitude toward learning, chances are the information will not stick with you. Therefore, you will not have a desire to apply what you learned.

For example, when taking a course understand and know what you want to take-away before committing to it. Meaning, before walking into the classroom plan a guide in your mind of what is going to be in the course. If the course is not of interest to you, chances are you will become complacent (un-worried) regardless if you have to fulfill a requirement to graduate. It is in your best interest to obtain advanced information before engaging in any course.

Your attitude is the primary and front point of an arrow to pierce any issues when it comes to a course being complicated, dull, or information that is too voluminous (large). When you approach any class with a positive attitude, you will do well. Let's take Calculus for instance; if you convince yourself before taking the course that it's not your subject, or you don't understand math, then you have already set yourself up for a difficult time.

Now it's time for you to take the course and the professor or teacher likes to emphasize that their class is challenging to scare students and to assert their superior understanding over them. Now the odds in your mind are lowering your chances of getting a favorable grade.

The key to passing what some perceive to be a problematic class like Calculus: knowing algebraic expressions, reviewing your information ahead of time, asking questions during lecture, and practicing the homework.  Remember, a teacher cannot test you on something that is not covered in your coursework.

In the past I took Pre-Calculus, I found that the teacher used intimidating tactics (create fear) on the students then showed a sense of pride on the last day when students withdrew.  In essence, he still got paid and at the same time felt a sense of intellectual superiority because 50% of the class withdrew.

On the other hand, I decided to study ahead using the course syllabus and became the professor's worst nightmare.  I somehow sensed a level of dishonesty in how he was teaching and what was being put on the exam (to give students that sense of inferiority).  So I studied and completed all the homework assignments, which was helpful in understanding the information.  When I took his exam, I did my best to recall the questions that were difficult, and the ones not covered in class or the homework.  After the exam, he would issue the grades and some of the students head's slump, indicating who failed.  As for me, I would generally ask him about a particular exam question and when it was covered during the lectures.  He would give me a blank stare and instructed me to see him after class.  At the end of class, he would try to insult my intelligence by stating, *"The question you are addressing... you should have learned in College Algebra."*  Then he would rush off without answering my original question.

I knew it!  He was projecting the problem on me while evading (avoiding) the question to give a false impression that the course was difficult when it wasn't.  To be honest, I got a B+ in the class; that's because he still refuses to this day to tell me where the information was in the homework and lectures that magically ended up on his exam.

The purpose of telling you this is to let you know that you can learn whatever you want to learn, regardless of your aptitude (talent).  It's all a matter of having a positive attitude, patience, and *will* to learn.  Focus your energy on your subjects, nothing is too difficult to learn, unless you convince yourself otherwise (or allow others to convince you).

Here is a little trick that helps a lot of kids learn; think of being Tom Cruise in the movie, *"Mission Impossible"* who somehow snuck into a classroom to learn what is being taught. You could even keep the tune of mission impossible in your head as the teacher instructs. Take notes, recall examples and apply what you learn. You can entertain yourself by making each day an adventure, especially when it comes to learning.

Just remember, you can't be tested on material that was not covered in a course. If that is occurring, you have grounds for a complaint to higher authorities.

You have a mind, you can learn anything even rocket science, but you have to have a will to learn it. There is nothing too complicated on this earth to understand, especially if man created it. I for one have called on the Lord to give me understanding, and the Holy Spirit was present to give me understanding. But the key, I had to demonstrate a will to learn.

Allow me to repeat it, "There is nothing too difficult on this earth to learn, especially when God is in your corner. Don't psych yourself out, psych yourself up!" The knowledge of this earth and the things within it are nowhere in comparison to God who is in control of it all.

To summarize, this portion of the chapter, have a positive attitude when it comes to learning. Seek to obtain all knowledge and information to glorify God better, and look to serve your fellow brethren. Set your goals high, expect to be a leader sent by God in the career field you have chosen; where you own and control what you do, or will do.

## As For School

School is an institution where information is handed out every single day it's in session. The question you must answer is whether you are completely taking advantage of the information being given?

If your answer is Yes, then you are accomplishing your role and mission as a student and later on in life an effective leader and teacher. Another vital component of school is that it can be a place to help develop good habits (i.e., study habits). Once you train yourself to tackle assignments and information immediately, it will be hard for the habit to leave you. For example, if you are given a reading assignment, math homework, or science project, do nothing concerning television or playing outside until you complete the required work. Studying when you are supposed to and ahead of schedule will foster good study habits that will last well into your retirement years.

How you view school, the grades you receive, and how it applies to real life is all tied together. Let's start with a simple job like working for a fast food restaurant. Your job is to make cheeseburgers. While at work, you are putting a cheeseburger together for a customer (sounds menial, but it's not to your customer). You cook the beef patties, add the cheese, put it on a bun; but forget the ketchup, lettuce, and tomatoes. What type of grade would you give yourself? (Hmmm, possibly 70 or 80 percent? Not bad because that is following most school standards). However, what type of grade would the customer give you? Especially when they know what's supposed to be on the cheeseburger? Chances are it would get sent back, indicating you failed. That's right, a customer expects 100 percent satisfaction, which 90, 85, and especially 70 percent is unacceptable.

Further, you may think that making cheeseburgers is for losers, but go into your favorite fast food restaurant and see how you flip out when they get an order wrong. That's why it's essential to build good habits that strive for 100 percent all the time. Start everything with an attitude that you are going to produce 100 percent no matter what course you are taking or job you are doing.

Let's look at a more complex career, like a surgeon. In this example, the surgeon is going to remove a cancerous tumor from a patient. He makes sure the person is sedated (sleep) then only cuts 70 percent of the cancerous growth out of their body when he could have cut 100 percent of it. What is the patient's reaction to him, when he/she wakes up, and he advises him/her of this…? Let me guess; they are livid (angry) because he got paid to do a thorough job, but did not do it because he left 30 percent of the tumor behind. Now the patient is going to have to come back for a second surgery. The patient asks, "Why didn't he remove 100 percent of the tumor?" The Surgeon explains, he did not have the will or desire. Plus, the nurses were telling him he was no good at his job and should only remove 70 percent of the tumor instead of 100 percent. Get the idea…?

School is a chance to get and give a 100 percent each day. Why not make it a habit to ensure that the rest of your learning years are easy? Put God and education first, then athletics, socializing, and the opposite sex second. Use school as a place to build habits that produce 100 percent positive results. In short, we all know we prefer a doctor who saves 100 percent of his patients' lives, and a lawyer who wins 100 percent of his clients' cases. To obtain this positive reputation (record), it starts with good learning habits that stay throughout an individual's schooling and career.

**Understand Your Teachers**

Contrary to the pre-calculus professor I introduced earlier; there are some teachers out there with a genuine interest and desire to teach. One can quickly identify them by the spark in their eye and enthusiasm (passion) in their voice when they teach. They are the complete opposite of teachers who are there because of: tenure, looking to collect a pension, just miserable and hate students, and the only pleasure they get is failing students.

Well, a majority of teachers who start a teaching career are very energetic with a great deal of drive and enthusiasm in the beginning. However, understand that most teachers' ambitions are sucked out of them by unappreciative students, hyper-critical parents, insignificant state guidelines, insatiable supervisors, and out of touch administrators.
To help your teacher help you, let them know now and then how much they are appreciated, and how they make a subject interesting. Another way to demonstrate this is by earning high grades through exams and assignments. Most teachers crave the appreciation of their students, more than from supervisors, peers or administrators. To be honest, that is why most teachers become teachers, to know that they made a difference in a student's life. Why not be that student who tells them how much they are appreciated and demonstrate the same by producing good grades (?).

To aid in your understanding of teachers, imagine yourself having to stand in front of the class, giving an oral presentation (sounds uncomfortable). Now stop and think about your peers interrupting you, making noise, not paying attention, just being outright disruptive (unpleasant and rude, wouldn't one think?) These are the things that help suck the enthusiasm out of a vibrant (lively) teacher who had good intentions of making a difference in someone's life. So do yourself and the teacher a favor by identifying those students/peers that are not looking to learn, and remove yourself from their surroundings. Their negativity and distractions are not only contagious (spread) but will take away your opportunity to receive information and build good learning habits.

The reality is, your teacher has a job to do and gets paid for it. As for you, what you economically earn in the future depends on the job performance you do in school each day. If you understand what your teacher is trying to accomplish, it makes learning easier. Also, it helps to build better social skills with authoritative figures that can help promote your career and access to information as you become an adult. So make it a habit of respecting and appreciating your educators, because the etiquette learned today will be a beneficial habit for tomorrow.

**Focus Is What We Need**

Here's a story I heard about a high school football player who slept, ate, and drank football. His grades in school were mediocre (average), which raised questions regarding his eligibility status on occasion; yet somehow he was able to pull out passing grades under stress.

It was the third game of the season, and he fractured his leg. His injury prevented him from playing football for the remainder of the season. All he could do was stand on the sidelines with a pathetic (sad) look that could never be quenched.

As a result of being out and on the sidelines, his focus turned more toward his books. He made the honor roll for the last three quarters of the school year. A significant number of people were shocked and could never comprehend how or why based on his past academic history.

However, it was simple; when the one thing that mattered most was taken he realized he had other options. Diverting (Redirecting) his focus on his books, he realized he had never entirely made use of his brain for anything other than football. It had become a barrier that consumed his entire thinking capacity.

Once the barrier was removed, he turned his focus to the only other thing happening in his life, school. He didn't have much of a social life because his earlier focus on football alienated (isolated) him from girls, who labeled him a maniac.

Having school work at his disposal, he just sat down and said, "Why not complete my homework or even read ahead of the class to understand the lectures?" This is a prime example of someone's focus being re-directed for the better.

The lesson here is managing all aspects of your life and distributing your focus evenly across the things you're passionate about or desire. Never possess one focus, spread your desires and wills across a spectrum (variety) of activities. Convince yourself that school is a primary focus. Gaining knowledge and creating good learning habits are vital to your future independence. Education is the key to living a more prosperous and comfortable life. To be without it will leave you vulnerable and reliable on others and their will. So, if you love yourself, do yourself a favor by learning all you can. The things to take from this chapter:

1. Learning is an attitude; if you have a *will*, you can learn anything.

2. School is an ideal place to build good habits.

3. It's not so much the subject/material; it's how you attack it.

4. Having a good work/ethic is profitable to the soul and wallet.

5. Train yourself to read ahead for the next lecture.

6. Understand your teacher's mission/goal.

7. Respecting teachers and their authority is proper training when dealing with future bosses.

8. Ask Questions.

9. Make school a priority that is why you are there.

   A significant part of your life's mission is school, so make the most of it. Take advantage of every bit of information given to you and savor it like your favorite dessert.

# Chapter 18 – After High School

There are plenty of colleges to choose from, as well as, various degree programs. The two levels of collegiate (college) study: undergraduate or graduate, if you decide to go that route. If college is not a goal, there are plenty of vocational schools to help perfect the skill or craft you may want to pursue. Just remember that after high school most of society does not expect anything from you other than to seek your career development and educational goals.

Most of the young people I encounter under the age of 22 put a great deal of emphasis on owning that nice new ride and putting rims on it so that they could be the envy of all who see them. However, reality reveals a few truths: some people will give you temporary praise, some will be envious for a little while, and the rest could care less.

Between the ages of 18 and 24 (building years), no one should have any expectations of you owning a nice car or lavish home. Although there's nothing wrong in having these items at a young age; be mindful that most people will presume (guess) that either mom or dad gave it to you. Also, that you engage in some illegal activity, or you won a lawsuit. In essence, owning these possessions at an early age leads people to the perception (insight) that you did not honestly earn what you possess. Nevertheless, it should not stop you from aspiring or acquiring these things, as long as it is within your means and you meet your career objectives. Question, "Do you want to get caught up in temporary materialistic (worldly) items that control you? Or do you want to get a more solid career to control the materialistic items you are a steward (manager) over?" Either way, don't worship things created by man's hands but seek a vocation (career) that provides services to glorify God and serve others.

With that being the question, do not be concerned with what others think or perceive about you during your building years. Focus on future economic stability and how you are going to take care of you and your family until you're no longer on the face of this earth.

Society's expectations of you being a successful adult at age 25. That is when people honestly ask, "What you do to obtain your means of survival (money)?" Whatever you choose, it should be something you enjoy, good at, and allows you to live the lifestyle you want to live. According to Confucius, *"Choose a job you love, and you will never have to work a day in your life."*

People who work to be wealthy find it to be somewhat of a hassle (trouble) when dealing with the problems that come with a considerable amount of money. The not so monetarily (money) driven, they don't have a problem living a comfortable lifestyle where their bills are paid, and they can save a few dollars regularly.

In your quest to become an expert in the career you choose, you will discover that most people are quite complacent and do not like to read or find the answers for themselves. So, they hire others to accomplish this; that person could be you, the one who has put himself/herself in demand. This alone is justification for planning your educational goals and the type of schooling that will help build your knowledge base.

For those who want to go straight to vocational school like Truck Driving, Plumbing, Electrician, Mechanic, HVAC Technician, Culinary Arts, Carpentry, Beautician, or Welding. Right after high school is the best time to start, because you still have a school mentality that will help you with the academics (school work).

As for those going to college (undergraduate) and choosing a degree program, there are two types of degrees: Impact Degrees and Support Degrees.

Impact Degrees are found in the following majors (Direct):

Engineering (Aeronautics, Biological, Chemical, Civil, Computer, Electrical, Mechanical, and Software)
Science (Biology, Chemistry, and Physics)
Mathematics
Architecture
Education
Computer Science
Information Technology
Medical – Pre-Med - Nursing
Physics

Support Degrees are the following (Indirect):

Accounting/Finance/Economics
Psychology
Sociology (Anthropology)
Theology (Spiritually Impactful)
Political Science
Criminal Justice
English
Business Administration
Entertainment - Music/Dance
Fashion Design
Film & Video
General Business
Humanities/History/Philosophy
Liberal Arts
Interior Design
International Studies
Marketing
Photography/Journalism/Broadcasting
Archeology

There are plenty of other degrees not mentioned. With an Impact Degree and appropriate electives, you are more likely to be in a position to go into various careers or upgrade with ease into Law School, Medical School, or Graduate School. Further, your field of study is in the higher tiers when it comes to salaries. With an Impact Degree, it is easier to get a career related to both (Direct and In-direct) occupations, than for someone with a Support Degree to obtain a career with a Direct occupation. By having an Impact Degree, your options are more significant when it comes to working in career paths other than the degree you obtained. For example, you can be an Engineer with a couple of minor classes in Education then go and be a Teacher. However, it is difficult (not impossible) for someone with a degree in Education to become an Engineer.

The crown jewel of any Nation is the need for more people with Impact Degrees to maintain our innovative dominance (invention control). Pursuing Impact Degrees takes our nation's heavy reliance off of other countries who know these degrees are vital to a country's success and security. In other words, it would decrease our dependency on other countries for goods and services in the future, while maintaining our competitive edge.

To be well-rounded, take electives that may interest you, either Impact or Support. However, the pursuit of an Impact Degree is more vital because mostly everyone wants to make an impact in this world.

Things to extract (take-away) from this chapter:

1. Know the significance of pursuing the right Degree or Vocational Training. Know the salary and career fulfillment.

2. Pursue your career with tenacity (persistence).

3. If you're going to college, know the long-term benefits of the Degree you are seeking.

# Chapter 19 – Your Future - Careers and Goals

There are myriads (a significant number) of people between the ages of 14 to 50 that don't know what to do with their lives. To be honest, I use to be one of them. Nonetheless, my life's experience has helped me to understand more about other careers. My exposure on how to get there is based on the people I have encountered, because of the multiple types of jobs I've held myself.

The important thing about making a career decision is to prioritize (arrange in order) on what would make you happy (money, job satisfaction, and so forth). Well, plenty of people would choose money; because most believe this will lead to more time for yourself, family, friends, and the things you enjoy doing. However, that is not necessarily 100% true. Some people who have money get into the rat race of pursuing more money, for others and themselves. A good percentage of people despise what they do for a living because it monopolizes (dominate) their time.

On the flip side, you can pick a career seeking job satisfaction. However, that may not help to pay the bills right away unless you are a successful athlete, musician, or actor.

Not knowing what career path to choose is common amongst a majority of young people in America. The cause stems from a lack of exposure to various jobs. Allow me to break things down into three categories on how one can work for their financial security: Owning a business; work for a company or government, or participate in an illegal activity that could risk one's life and liberty. For the sake of this chapter, we will discuss only the first two categories. The top 21 careers for today and tomorrow that could help you towards your financial goals of owning your own home, cars, retiring early, and vacationing whenever and wherever you want (Information from various 2015 to 2017 career sources):

## **Doctor:**

**Goal:** Own a hospital or practice or an Attending Physician with a local hospital. Approximate Starting Salary: $60,000 a year.

**Pros:** Ability to heal or comfort those in need of medical attention. Help restore those who have been damaged by disease or injury.

**Cons:** The cost of undergraduate college and medical school. (8 years) Internship - where you earn little money to pay off student loans while you learn and practice. May take several years to establish a good reputation; plus, any severe malpractice could ruin a career. Work can interrupt and monopolize your free time. Dealing with health insurance, bureaucracies, and the high cost of Malpractice Insurance can drain you.

**Steps:** Standardized Test: SAT or ACT (Scholastic Assessment Test - American College Test) before undergraduate college. Taking the MCAT (Medical College Admission Test) exam during ($4^{th}$ year) or after undergraduate college. Then required Medical Board Exams after Medical School.

**School:** Undergraduate - Bachelors of Science Degree and preferable course study in Pre-med, Biology, Physiology, Chemistry, Nursing, Mortuary Science, Anatomy, Math & Engineering. Graduate School – Medical School (four (4) years or more).

**Work:** Internship in specialty, Residency specialization, and Practitioner (Attending Physician) in a field of study (Orthopedic, Neurology, Emergency, Internal, Radiology, Oncology, Pediatric, etc…).

**Traits:** Detail oriented, love of science (Biology, Anatomy, Physiology, & Chemistry) and curiosity about what makes people physically tick.

## Lawyer:

**Goal:** Own a practice, partnership, be a judge or politician. Approximate Starting Salary: $60,000 a year.

**Pros:** Flexibility in career choice. Intellectual challenges with the ability to foster positive change: locally, nationwide, and globally.

**Cons:** The cost of Undergraduate College and Law School. (7 years). The time it takes to establish a good reputation, which mistakes could blemish your career. Interacting with some antiquated judges and unreasonable clients to earn a living. Work can monopolize your free time.

**Steps:** Standardized Test: SAT or ACT before undergraduate college. Taking the LSAT (Law School Admission Test) exam during ($4^{th}$ year), or after undergraduate school. Then take the State Bar-Exams after Law School graduation.

**School:** Undergraduate – Bachelor of Arts or Science (any discipline), or preferable course study: Criminal Justice, Political Science, Engineering, Chemistry, Biology, Mathematics, Humanities, Sociology, Psychology, History, Accounting, Finance, and Marketing. Graduate School - Attend three (3) year Law School.

**Work:** Internships while in Undergraduate and Law School is helpful. Work for a law firm or government to build experience and reputation. Decide on a specialty in law, (Corporate, Civil, Criminal, Family, Estates, Intellectual Property, Real Estate, etc...).

**Traits:** Detailed oriented, logical, problem solver, good at being persuasive. Don't mind a good argument or debate.

## Engineer/Scientist/Chemist/Computers:

**Goal:** Create an invention; own an engineering firm, work for a private company, defense contractor, or government. Approximate Starting Salary: 50,000 a year.

**Pros:** At the cutting edge of technology and ingenuity. Instant millionaire if you create a great invention.

**Cons:** Possible 4 years of undergraduate college (Optional graduate school for Masters or Ph.D.) Extensive research and development that can lead to failed projects.

**Steps:** Standardized Test: SAT or ACT before undergraduate college. Take the GMAT (Graduate Management Admission Test) or GRE (Graduate Record Examination) during (4$^{th}$ year) or after undergraduate. Obtain appropriate certifications, if applicable.

**School:** Undergraduate - Bachelor Degree and coursework: Mathematics, Algebra, Calculus, Sciences, Chemistry, Biology, Physics, Engineering disciplines: Mechanical, Electrical, Biological, Aeronautics, Chemical, Civil, Computers, and Software. Prep in high school by taking algebra, pre-calculus, chemistry, physics, and biology.

**Work:** Internships throughout college. Expect continuous learning as your peers produce new inventions. Obtain advanced degrees for credibility and enhance knowledge. Optional: Try to get into a National Security Agency (NSA) approved college or Approved Board Engineering Technology (ABET).

**Traits:** Detailed oriented, desire to know how things work, love for science and to create new products from raw material or enhance existing products.

## Pilot:

**Goal:** Own your own airline company, become a Flight Captain, or fly for the military (8-year minimum commitment). Approximate Starting Salary: $70,000 a year.

**Pros:** Travel domestically or internationally, more days off during the week. Good pay for both commercial and military.

**Cons:** Half of your career spent in other cities and not at home. Cost of pilot training, or go through the Military (ROTC during college, Officer School Post College - Boot camp before receiving formal pilot training). Cost for a license, unless you go the military route, you will owe eight years. Commercial airlines have unexpected furloughs (Temporary layoffs).

**Steps:** Standardized Test: SAT or ACT before undergraduate college, Military Officer Exam during or after college. Obtain Private pilot license – single engine, multi-engine, and commercial under FAA guidance.

**School:** Undergraduate - Obtain Bachelor Degree, preferably studies in Aeronautics, Aviation, Engineering, Mathematics, Chemistry, and Physics. Or, any type of degree and apply for a military pilot position.

**Work:** Fly Second chair as a co-pilot, then become the pilot. Or, go to commercial pilot airline school mostly located in Florida or Arizona.

**Traits:** Desire to fly, navigation, math, and speed.

## Professional Athlete:

**Goal:** Be well known and outstanding performer, Hall of Fame in sport, coach, owner of a team. Approximate Starting Salary: $200,000 a year

**Pros:** Enjoying what you do with the potential of receiving fame if you're successful. Travel to different cities. Time off during the off-season.

**Cons:** Worry about injuries that could threaten your career. Must manage money to prepare for an unfortunate event, or if you're cut from the team. Someone is always after your spot. Dealing with insatiable fans.

**Steps:** Standardized Test: SAT or ACT before undergraduate college.

**School:** Undergraduate – Study any discipline, but focus on business courses, sports injuries, and physical therapy.

**Work:** Practice hard in the sport you like. Do your best in college and on the playing field. A positive attitude is essential.

**Traits:** Natural ability in sport, love, and dedication for the position, or positions you play.

## Investment Banker/Broker, Accountant, or Stockbroker:

**Goal:** Own a firm, have clients with large accounts and retire early. Approximate Starting Salary: $60,000 a year

**Pros:** Helping others earn money or obtain financial independence. You accomplish this by monitoring and projecting; market and investment trends.

**Cons:** Lots of studying, just as fast as you can earn money, you can lose it even quicker. Need to build large clientele as an Investment Broker/Banker and Accountant.

**Steps:** Standardized Test: SAT or ACT before undergraduate college. Take the CPA or License Exam after college or corporate training program. High School Diploma to be a stockbroker (College Optional), pass the appropriate series exam.

**School:** Undergraduate - Pursue Bachelors in Finance, Economics, Marketing, Advertisement, and Accounting.

**Work:** Build clientele and book of business. Build a reputation and know what your customers like and dislike.

**Traits:** Love of numbers and economics with an ability to predict market trends.

## Law Enforcement/EMS/Military

**Goal:** Become a leader, Chief, Sheriff, Warden, Marshal, Director, Officer, and Senior Non-Commissioned Officer. Start own security firm or be a consultant, work for a defense contractor. Approximate Starting Salary: $30,000 a year.

**Pros:** Public Service and exercise authority. Retire in 20 to 30 years. Overtime, Pension, and Travel are some excellent benefits.

**Cons:** Dangerous work at times, dealing with people who may not favor your presence or those who want to do you harm, uncontrolled work schedule. Travel to undesirable places and austere conditions.

**Steps:** Standardized Test: Civil Service Exam, College Optional for some local departments. If undergraduate college, prepare for SAT or ACT. Military Aptitude Exam for military training and career exposure.

**School:** Obtain High School Diploma, know math, vocabulary, science, writing, and reading comprehension (mainly for the understanding of the law and requirements) for the civil service exam. Some college is required for certain law enforcement jobs, but mandatory degrees for employment with the FBI, US Marshals, State, and Federal Probation. To become an Officer in the Military, a degree along with taking the Military Officer Aptitude exam. So prep for SAT while in High School if the latter part of these steps is your goal.

**Work:** On the job training after graduating appropriate academy.

**Traits:** Take charge attitude, interpersonal skills, investigative mind, and strong communication skills.

## Journalist/Writer/Broadcaster

**Goal:** Own a newspaper, publishing company, or TV network. Become Chief Editor or Chief Program Director. Retire early. Approximate Starting Salary: $35,000 a year.

**Pros:** Being at the forefront of a story as it develops. Decision making on what information gets read or seen by the public.

**Cons:** Dealing with pressing deadlines, uncooperative people, insatiable supervisors, and critical information consumers (audience).

**Steps:** Standardized Test: SAT or ACT before undergraduate college. Taking the GMAT or GRE during the $4^{th}$ year of college; if planning on obtaining a graduate degree.

**School:** Undergraduate - Bachelor Degree or course study in English, Journalism, Broadcasting, Sociology, Public Relations, and History.
**Work:** Prepare to accomplish an internship to build experience in this fast pace career.
**Traits:** Investigative mind, strong communication skills, a love for words. Descriptive verbally and in writing, excellent storytelling skills.

## Electrician/Plumber/Carpenter/Mechanic/Truck Driver

**Goal:** Own Business (Retail, Distributor, or Direct Work), Network with other Contractors. Approximate Starting Salary: $40,000 a year.
**Pros:** Ability to work with your hands and job satisfaction upon completion of any project.
**Cons:** Work in confined places and possibly poor conditions, weather dictates if you work, or not. Backlog on clientele could hurt your reputation and future jobs, study for appropriate licenses with fees.
**Steps:** Standardized Test: College optional therefore SAT or ACT are optional. Complete mandatory license exam in the career field.
**School:** High School Diploma, Study trade while in High School with Shop Classes, if applicable. Go to Vocational/Technical/Trade school with job placement for basic knowledge and hands-on experience.
**Work:** Look for apprenticeship and study for the necessary license before or during apprenticeship. Look to network with larger contract firms until you own a large contract firm.
**Traits:** Love to work with hands, good hand and eye coordination, love for measurements, understand how things are built and how they work. Ability to follow instructions, read blueprints, and read directions.

## Insurance (Sales, Claims, Underwriting):

**Goal:** Own your own company, brokerage firm, or third party administration firm. Approximate Starting Salary: $40,000 a year.

**Pros:** Interfacing with the public; selling or providing financial security for clientele.

**Cons:** Takes time to build clientele and relationships, time to work one's way up the corporate ladder. May encounter corporate glass ceilings where nepotism and cronyism are prevalent. Work long and hard hours/days for little recognition without overtime. Complete reports for investors and senior management.

**Steps:** Standardized Test: Prep for SAT or ACT (college may be optional, but helpful in getting through the door.). License exams for Agent, Brokers, and Adjuster (depends on State requirements).

**School:** High School Diploma. Undergraduate - Obtain college degree or course study in Finance, Marketing, Accounting, Criminal Justice, Insurance, Economics, and Mathematics. Additional internal training and certifications may be required.

**Work:** Actuary, Underwriting, Claims, Broker's Office or Agency.

**Traits:** Strong interpersonal skills, investigative mind, ability to be persuasive, mathematically inclined, with negotiation skills.

## Teacher/Professor/Education Admin:

**Goal:** Own a private school, become a Head Administrator of a school district, or Principal of a School, or enjoy teaching a class. Approximate Starting Salary: $30,000 a year.

**Pros:** Training young and bright minds, summers off, along with holidays. Retire in 20 to 30 years.

**Cons:** Dealing with disruptive students, possibly insatiable supervisors, and administrators. Comply with state guidelines for education. Grade papers and tests, bringing work home.

**Steps:** Standardized Test: SAT or ACT and Teacher Certification, GMAT and GRE for Graduate School (Masters or Doctorate).

**School:** Undergraduate - Obtain a Degree in Education, or any other Major (sciences, math, history, political science) with the necessary state educational credits, which varies for each state.
**Work:** Internship as a student teacher, then as a teacher. Certification testing required for a majority of states.
**Traits:** Interpersonal skills, patience, high level of tolerance, good storyteller skills, desire to teach, open mind, an excellent orator, and problem solver.

## Nurse:

**Goal:** Become a Registered Nurse (RN), be a head nurse at a hospital or healthcare facility, be a consultant, or own your own business. Approximate Starting Salary: $50,000 a year
**Pros:** Feeling of satisfaction when you provide care and comfort for those in need. Retire in 20 to 30 years.
**Cons:** Uncontrolled work schedule, depression when dealing with the loss of those who don't recover. Forced to possibly interact with some callous: Doctors, Hospital and Office Administrators, and Health Insurance Companies in your day to day activities.
**Steps:** Standardized Test: SAT or ACT before undergraduate college. Take the GMAT or GRE if looking to go to graduate school (Masters or Doctorate). Pass Registered Nurse (RN) exam after graduation.
**School:** Undergraduate - Obtain college degree in Nursing, if you elect to go further, become a professor or teacher in nursing.
**Work:** At a Hospital, Nursing Home, or School.
**Traits:** Compassionate, empathetic, caring, and nurturing.

## Real Estate/Mortgage Brokers:

**Goals:** Own Real Estate or Mortgage Firm, Become a Developer. Approximate Starting Salary: $60,000 a year

**Pros:** Feeling of satisfaction when placing people in the right home. Excellent commissions and perks.
**Cons:** Dealing with insatiable clients, fluctuating real estate market, licenses, and exams.
**Steps:** College is optional, therefore SAT or ACT is optional. Obtain appropriate license in Real Estate – Depends on State requirements.
**School:** College Degree (optional, but Helpful). Study Economics, Accounting, Marketing, Mathematics, Science, Architecture, Drafting, and Business.
**Work:** Work for Agency or Brokerage Firm. Network and market your skills. Know real estate appraisals and title searches.
**Traits:** Interpersonal skills, empathetic, persuasive, stylish, charming, and mathematical.

## Architecture/Drafting/Design:

**Goals:** Own a firm, become a partner, management in a firm or government. Approximate Starting Salary: $65,000 a year
**Pros:** Ability to express creativity and enhance the images/structures surrounding humankind.
**Cons:** Dealing with unrealistic clients that may have escrow issues, some complacent general contractors and subcontractors, missed deadlines, municipal building permits, and latent structural defects.
**Steps:** Standardized Test: SAT or ACT before undergraduate college. GMAT or GRE for graduate studies (Masters or Doctorate). Complete appropriate licenses.
**School:** Undergraduate Studies: Architecture, Drafting or Interior Design. Prepare for college by studying sciences and mathematics: Geology Topography, Meteorology, Landscaping, Chemistry, Physics, Drafting, Algebra, and Calculus. Maybe a five (5) year degree program (depends on college); advanced degree may help with credibility and networking.
**Work:** Internships to develop skills as an Architect.

**Traits:** Artistic, creative, understand math and science; then apply them.

## Pharmacist:

**Goals:** Own a Pharmacy or Pharmaceutical Company, or be a Manager at a Drug Store. Approximate Starting Salary: $80,000 a year.
**Pros:** Provide services that enhance the quality of life for others.
**Cons:** Up to 6 years of college with internships, one mistake or oversight could jeopardize someone's life and your career.
**Steps:** Standardized Test: SAT or ACT before undergraduate college. Take the GMAT, MCAT, or GRE for a Masters or Doctorate Degree. Complete required licensing exam.
**School:** Undergraduate - Obtain a Degree in Pharmacy. To prepare for college coursework; study math and sciences (chemistry, biology, anatomy, and physiology).
**Work:** Internships with Pharmaceutical Companies.
**Traits:** Strong understanding of Chemistry, Biology, Anatomy, and Physiology.

## Politician:

**Goal:** Run for office and stay in office, or escalate to a higher office. Approximate Starting Salary: $50,000 a year.
**Pros:** Public recognition and notoriety. Solve problems and affect public policy.
**Cons:** Can be voted out of office, can only please some of your constituents (voters), long hours and extremely busy during election season.
**Steps:** Standardized Exam: College is optional but vital for credibility. Complete the SAT or ACT before undergraduate college. Take the GMAT, GRE, and LSAT for Graduate/Law School.
**School:** Undergraduate - Obtain College Degree in Political Science, Criminal Justice, Philosophy, Humanities, Liberal Science,

Psychology, Sociology, Business Management, Accounting, Economics, Marketing, and Education.

**Work:** Locate electoral rules and regulations for the office you are running for, network, and then campaign.

**Traits:** Charismatic, Good Orator, Problem Solver, Prognosticator, Empathetic, Sympathetic, and Servant for the Public.

## Retail/Sales:

**Goal:** Own a store, or become a store manager. Approximate Starting Salary: $25,000 a year

**Pros:** Providing goods and services to the public and dictate the products you wish to sell.

**Cons:** Poor monthly sales, insatiable customers, markdowns, sales, inventory, and low commission.

**Steps:** Standardized Test: College is optional therefore SAT, or ACT is optional. Take the GMAT and GRE for graduate school.

**School:** College is optional but helpful in obtaining a Manager's position: Degree in Business, Marketing, Advertisement, Economics, Finance, and Accounting.

**Work:** Department Stores or Corporate Offices that focus on Retail.

**Traits:** Customer oriented, non-argumentative, develop a belief in the product(s) you are selling.

## Marketing/Advertising:

**Goal:** Own a firm, become an executive or manager. Approximate Starting Salary: $40,000 a year.

**Pros:** Exercise your creativity, the ability to see your ideas turn into reality that generates a profit.

**Cons:** Tight deadlines, insatiable clients, un-cooperative contractors and subcontractors, long hours, and detailed accounting.

**Steps:** Standardized Test: SAT or ACT before undergraduate college. Take the GMAT or GRE if looking to obtain a Graduate Degree (Masters or Doctorate).
**School:** Undergraduate - Obtain college degree in Marketing, Advertisement, Accounting, Economics, Finance, Art and Design, Business, Management, Sociology, and Psychology.
**Work:** Internship with Marketing and Advertising Firms.
**Traits:** Creativity, good sense of humor, a good orator, persuasive, entertaining, proper etiquette, and a good understanding of society.

**Government/Air Traffic Control:**

**Goal:** Manager or Director, member of Senior Executive Staff, Retire in 20 to 30 years. Approximate Starting Salary: $65,000 a year
**Pros:** Creator and implementer of government policy to better serve the public.
**Cons:** Regulations to comply with a high-stress job because other people's lives are in your hand. Watching bleeps on a monitor every day you're at work.
**Steps:** Standardized Exam: Air Traffic Control Exam after high school. SAT or ACT is optional because college is optional. Military Aptitude Exam to get on the job training.
**School:** Optional College, but if expecting to make it to Senior Executive Staff, it will be required. A degree can be in any major or minor. High School Diploma (Prep for Civil Service exams Air Traffic Control).
**Work:** Military training or direct federal training after passing exams.
**Traits:** Good follower and leader; understand rules and ability to apply the rules, understand radar theory, problem-solving skills, good radio communicator, and interpersonal skills.

**Photographer/Graphics/Artist/Dancer/Actor/Cinematography:**

**Goal:** Own a studio and establish a reputation for producing good work. Approximate Starting Salary: $30,000 a year.
**Pros:** Enjoy what you do, obtain notoriety, and respect for your craft.
**Cons:** Struggle at first to get recognition and sponsorship. Sacrifice certain pleasure and desires to fulfill dreams. Watch out for corrupt individuals looking to take advantage of you. May have to work as an understudy or apprentice with little or no salary.
**Steps:** Standardized Test: College is optional therefore SAT, or ACT is optional.
**School:** Undergraduate – Study Art and Photography or attend a vocational school in your specialty.
**Work:** Be an apprentice or understudy. Willingness to immediately network with peers, producers, and directors.
**Traits:** Talent in an area of interest, persistent, resourceful in knowing where the jobs are. Learn how to be convincing and influential. Project optimism and confidence at all times.

## Bishop/Pastor/Reverend/Minister:

**Goals:** Influential spiritual leader, Shepard over a church, establish a faithful congregation. Approximate Starting Salary: $30,000 a year.
**Pros:** Doing the Lord's work, counseling members, helping others, strengthening your spiritual growth.
**Cons:** Dealing with defiant members. Managing the church's business, that can test your faith. Economics may be a little low, and when starting-out this will most likely be a part-time position.
**Steps:** Standardized Test: College is Optional therefore SAT, or ACT is optional. If going for an advanced Degree GMAT or GRE may be required.
**School:** Undergraduate - Degree in Theology, if not any field. Be ordained and attend seminary school.
**Work:** As an associate minister or assistant minister before branching out on your own.

**Traits:** Love of the Lord and his written word. Also, have multiple characteristics: peacemaker, humble, meek, good listener, a good orator, charismatic, and persuasive.

These are the top twenty-one careers of successful people who have obtained some enjoyment in what they do; I'm sure there are other careers I have not mentioned. The key to outlining this was to give some exposure to various professions. Also, point out potential starting salaries, pros, cons, and steps in achieving your career goals.

When I was 17 years old, I was not exposed to the salaries, pros, cons, and steps of any career. Plus, I could vividly remember people asking me before graduation, "What are you going to do with your life…?" I had no clue because I never had any real career exposure. At the time, the only jobs I knew of were in fast food and being a summer-time janitor.

With the multiple careers I've held since then, I wish I could go back in time with what I know now; to tell myself what degree and career to work. Then re-focus my energy on certain subjects. Most parents are supportive of their children's goal and take a backseat by saying, "I'm going to let them do what they want to do… I'm not going to get involved." The truth is some kids don't know what to do for a career. If they have an idea, they are not sure of the steps that will take them there.

If there is no family-owned business or the child does not wish to participate in a family-owned business (where a child can receive direct career exposure); then a parent must find out about a child's interest. After a parent understands a child's desire for a career, research should be conducted on that particular career field. If the child or parent knows of someone working in the desired career field, they should seek an opportunity for the child to be mentored by that person.

In conclusion, I hope the information in this chapter will be helpful for anyone who reads it. Remember, what you do and what you want to do are all up to you. Attempt to get some exposure then prepare yourself with the time and free will God has given you to pursue your career goals.

# Chapter 20 - Intelligent Investments

In America and many other parts of the world, people are faced with the decision of what to do with their money on a daily basis. One must choose to spend money on things that "Appreciate" or "Depreciate."

1 Timothy 6:10 KJV: *"For the love of money is the root of all evil..."* With that being said, don't love money; instead, manage it. As sure as you are living, money will come and go, but to increase the amount that passes through your hands, manage it wisely. Always keep in mind that you can't take your money with you when you depart this earth.

Now, is that a good reason to be careless with the money you earn? Money is an object of this world and is used to purchase services and materialistic needs/wants. So what are things you can invest in today that will appreciate over time? To be succinct:

1. God
2. Health
3. Education
4. Real Estate
5. Retirement Accounts.

If you must go into debt, remember there is good debt and bad debt. Now you're probably thinking, "What's the difference... debt is always a bad thing?" Agreed, but not entirely true, there's an old common expression, *"To make money, you have to spend it."* Therefore, if you decide to spend it or go into debt, make a choice towards something that will "Appreciate."

First, it is always a good thing to invest in God. Spending time and money toward the things important (spread Gospel and being of service) to the Lord are commendable and exceeds the rewards of this world, especially if you are a responsible steward and trusting in God's word for blessings to overflow in your life. Bring your tithes and offerings to a church that is genuinely a storehouse (providing support to the priests, widows, fatherless, strangers, and support of Christ's gospel). The percentage is at least 10% of your time and money. To reiterate, the benefit in doing this shows your faith in God and that He will meet your every need because of your faithfulness.

> *"He that is faithful in that which is least is faithful also in much: and he that is unjust in the least is unjust also in much." (Luke 16:10 KJV)*

The antithesis (opposite) of not giving to God and the symbolic end-results can are found in Haggai 1:3-11:

> *"Then came the word of the Lord by Haggai the prophet, saying, Is it time for you, O ye, to dwell in your ceiled houses, and this house lie waste? Now therefore thus saith the Lord of hosts; Consider your ways. Ye have sown much, and bring in little; ye eat, but ye have not enough; ye drink, but ye are not filled with drink; ye clothe you, but there is none warm; and he that earneth wages earneth wages to put it into a bag with holes. Thus saith the Lord of hosts; Consider your ways. Go up to the mountain, and bring wood, and build the house; and I will take pleasure in it, and I will be glorified, saith the Lord. Ye looked for much, and, lo it came to little; and when ye brought it home, I did blow upon it. Why? saith the Lord of hosts. Because of mine house that is waste, and ye run every man unto his own house. Therefore the heaven over you is stayed from dew, and the earth is stayed from her fruit. And I called for a drought upon the land, and upon the mountains, and upon the corn, and upon the new wine, and upon the oil, and upon that which the ground bringeth forth, and upon men, and upon cattle, and upon all the labour of the hands." (KJV)*

The next best thing to invest in is your Health, just as it was pointed out in Chapter 12. It is essential to spend money on eating right and exercising your body. With the rising cost of healthcare, do your body a favor by maintaining a healthy lifestyle by eating right and spending time exercising. In essence, if you're not healthy, all other endeavors are insignificant except your relationship with God, family, and friends.

Third, investing in an Education is something that will benefit your future because the value of it appreciates over time. Having an education empowers you to make informed decisions (not 100 percent correct ones, but education tips the scale in your favor). Further, the price for college today will not be the same price tomorrow. Therefore, choose a major or field of study that helps to increase your knowledge and places yourself in demand, as expressed in the three previous chapters.

As for Real Estate, it is just like education, where the cost will not be the same today as tomorrow. Yes, a majority of real estate appreciates over-time. In most cases, equity in a home is accrued a few years after purchase; so it is in your best interest to own a home. Do your best to ensure it is comparable to your salary and allows you to save what you need. Look into purchasing other homes and leasing them out for additional cash flow. Remember having good credit is the key; because having it allows you to leverage yourself when you don't have the full amount of resources you require.

Lastly, investing in a stable Retirement Plan is essential as you progress toward your golden years. The last thing anyone wants is to be dependent on others, or working during their retirement years. Once you get your first job, meet with a Retirement Planner and look to set up diverse retirement accounts, such as Individual Retirement Accounts (IRA), Mutual Funds, Stocks and Bonds, Participate in Company 401K, and be appreciative if your job provides a Pension Program. Saving approximately Ten Percent (10%) or more of your income is beneficial to have a healthy retirement plan.

As for things that depreciate: credit card debt, car loans, and personal loans. Borrowing money for items and services that depreciate only allows businesses to get rich off of you.  Now I'm not saying don't use a credit card, because you may be placed in a position to use them.  Nonetheless, acquiring a single credit card to build your credit status/score is a good start (because not using your credit is the same as not having any credit or credit history).  However, do your best to avoid being dependent on credit cards by paying them off right away.  To reiterate, too much usage only benefits the credit card companies.  Why else would you see advertisements and receive solicitations in the mail for you to open up an account?  Once again, someone is getting rich off of you going into debt.  Practice being frugal and be knowledgeable of your needs and wants.  More importantly, build an emergency cash fund as soon as possible to avoid being dependent on a credit card.

    Ask yourself, when you see something at the store, "Is it a need or a want?"  If it is a need like food, water, shelter, or brakes for the car; it's a higher priority than wanting a new pair of sneakers (when you have another decent pair in your closet).  You can also break it down to things of vanity versus things that are essential.  Items of vanity only go to enhance an image you want to project, while things that are necessary help you to maintain and survive.  To help you prioritize, take a sheet of paper and split it into two columns.  List those things that are essential to the left and non-essential (vanity) to the right.  By doing this will help you remember and prioritize what is necessary.

    A verse that helps put this into perspective is found in Proverbs 12:11:

> "*He that tilleth his land shall be satisfied with bread: but he that followeth vain persons is void of understanding.*" *(KJV)*

The key things to pull from this chapter:

1. Identify things that appreciate: God, Health, Education, Real Estate, & Retirement.

2. Recognize the things that depreciate.

3. Spend money wisely by prioritizing.

4. Know the difference between your needs and wants.

5. Know the difference between essential and non-essential purchases – list them out.

# Chapter 21 – Life's Storms

In life, there are many different types of storms. Some storms occur at different realms (areas): natural, social, financial, physical, and mental. The main thing about any storm, big or small, is that it comes to change things. It changes how we live or think, act or react, succumb or overcome. The only thing anyone can do is prepare for a storm and its aftermath.

Since Adam set things in disarray (out of order), these storms are inherent (natural) in this fallen world. So one thing is inevitable (going to happen), life is going to put some storms in our paths. The question is whether we can predict the type of storms we encounter, how we will manage during the storm, and how will we recover after it is over.

The most common storm humankind encounters are natural storms. This storm can be as small as a thunderstorm or as large as a hurricane. Nonetheless, it comes and changes things, either hardly noticeable to significant. To prepare for storms that will come and change the landscape of where one lives or the shelter we dwell in, it helps to have money (or at least insurance). Many people lose priceless things that are irreplaceable, like family heirlooms and memoirs. While they are never fully restored, often with insurance, one can be in a position to start over. Natural storms are mainly experienced by all who share a common geographic area. The effects or change could be short term, as well as, long-term. An example of a short-term effect is a ruined flowerbed, while an example of a long-term effect is Hurricane Katrina where the impact and damage affected peoples' lives at various levels (damaged houses, neighborhoods, and death).

As for social storms, these are the conflicts we encounter in our daily interactions with others: like family members, friends, employer/employees, co-workers, fellow students, teachers, or enemies. Storms in this realm (area) kick up when there is a conflict or difference of opinions. Some storms can be minor (like an argument) or major (like a physical altercation). Just like natural storms, social storms change individual's perspectives (view) of each other. It can damage or strengthen a relationship. But one thing is for sure out of any new conflict; new alliances and adversaries are formed. The questions one must ask their self:

1. Can I control myself by remaining faithful to God and myself during social conflicts?

2. Can I seek peace and maintain peace after a disagreement?

3. Can I walk away with a better understanding of all those who were engaged in such a conflict?

4. Will I fuel dissent and strife between all those involved?

5. Do I create my storms when I make poor choices?

Matthews 5:9:

*"Blessed are the peacemakers: for they shall be called the children of God" (KJV)*

To be a good peacemaker, know that communication between disagreeing parties is essential even if one or all sides are being irrational. To close communication between disagreeing parties will lead to speculations and fallacies that each side will conjure up (makeup) in the absence of having shared dialogue (which can only prolong a conflict).

To be a good peacemaker, you must allow all parties to openly communicate (even if it is your adversary) without concessions (surrendering). In that type of forum you may find out that your perceived adversary may not be your adversary after all, and a peaceful resolution (resolve) might be a blink of an eye away. It's never an intelligent act to restrain or close the door with any disagreeing parties; because you are ultimately suppressing or closing the door on peace.

As for financial storms, there are times when most people wrestle to obtain some economic advantage. These storms come to deplete our savings account: like the repairs for a car, medical expense, or unexpected funeral expense of a loved one. In general, financial storms come when we have unforeseen or unaffordable costs, or make a poor economic decision that can leave us in debt.

How does one prepare for unexpected expenses? Most financial advisors would recommend that we save ten (10) to twenty (20) percent of what we bring home. Plus, religious leaders encourage the practice of tithing (10 percent) as a form of trusting in God to supply all our needs. In essence, spending seventy (70) percent of what you net is a barometer for what is considered, "living within your means." We can all convince ourselves that anything above seventy 70 percent is considered outside of our means. To be truly prepared for an unforeseeable event is quite difficult. To help defray any future cost, look to purchase the appropriate insurance (including burial) or save for a rainy day. When individuals stray from planning or spend too much on buying lavishing (showering) materialistic items they can't afford is an example of people creating their own financial storm.

When dealing with physical storms, it refers to the things that happen to our bodies as we move through life; such as, minor or major injuries that can debilitate you for a short or long period of time, and diseases that can monopolize your health with a slow recovery or no recovery (including death). As expressed in Chapter 12 & 20, investing in your health is essential to living. However, there are still physical storms that can come and take away things we may take for granted: like the ability to get up and walk across a room; move an arm to reach for a newspaper; ability to hear music or see a beautiful sunset. No one ever misses what they can do, until the ability is gone.

Can you prepare for such an event? Do you even want to think about a physical storm like this occurring in your life or the lives of anyone you know? I don't.... Nonetheless, it still happens... and there is no real way to prepare for a physical storm that may arise from a fortuitous event, except condition your mind.

After an unfortunate event, Psychologists identify the mental phases people go through denial, anger, negotiation, depression, and finally acceptance of their circumstances. However, many overcome physical storms that can change a person's physical abilities by wrestling and winning the internal battle within themselves which brings us to the last realm, mental storms.

Mental agility is the most critical aspect of dealing with all storms. It starts with your psyche (inner self) and your willingness to overcome no matter what. In the mind is where your optimism (positive) battles your pessimism (negative); when your fear, logic, and knowledge of this world challenge your faith and belief in God. As for who will win? The answer rests within yourself.

Before anyone can even prepare, endure, or deal with the aftermath of a storm their mentality has to be either positive or negative. To set the pace on how one handles all the other types of storms (natural, physical, financial and social). Within the mental realm, the spiritual realm is either large or small; this is based on faith and knowledge of God's word. Indeed, the spiritual realm exists, and the size is contingent (depending) upon one having a God like mind that consumes one's mental realm. Being of a spiritual mind, one knows that there is no problem greater than God, and storms and trouble don't last always. Therefore, our minds are placed above all problems and storms that arise.

An excellent example that solidifies what is being conveyed can be found in the Bible and taken from, Matthew 14:24-32:

> *"But the ship was now in the midst of the sea, tossed with waves: for the wind was contrary. And in the fourth watch of the night Jesus went unto them, walking on the sea. And when the disciples saw him walking on the sea, they were troubled, saying, It is a spirit; and they cried out for fear. But straightway*

*Jesus spake unto them, saying, Be of good cheer, it is I; be not afraid. And Peter answered him and said, Lord, if it be thou; bid me come unto thee on the water. And he said, Come. And when Peter was come down out of the ship, he walked on the water, to go to Jesus. But when he saw the wind boisterous, he was afraid, and beginning to sink, he cried, saying, Lord, save me. And immediately Jesus stretched forth his hand, and caught him, O thou of little faith, wherefore didst thou doubt? And when they were come into the ship, the wind ceased." (KJV)*

The above symbolizes (represents) the internal battle man encounters while in the mental realm. Indeed, Jesus walking on water is a miracle, but He's Jesus. As for Peter, stepping out of the boat onto the water without sinking occurred because his faith/focus was on Christ. When Peter took his attention off of Christ (who was of a spiritual mind), by looking at the wind and water, he began to sink. In summary, his mind went back to the mental realm that focused on the problem, and not Christ.

Within our internal battles, the line is drawn between faith and doubt. When we believe more in our faith (God), we engage our spiritual side. When we doubt, we engage our worldly side.

The questions we can ask ourselves on a daily basis are: If a storm kicks up, will I focus on my circumstances or faith in God? Will I be able to maintain a spiritual mind that is Christ-like without wavering, no matter what changes may occur during a storm or thereafter?

In this life, there are many different types of storms that kick up. Like Peter, most people step out on faith but soon sink once they take their focus off of Christ and focus on the circumstances. A significant number of us do this and are submerged under the water and consumed by our problems. Then, some people are treading water with the ability to keep their head above water, or in this case above their current circumstances.

The beautiful thing about Christ is that with Him, we all can walk on water or above our circumstances. At the same time, we can serve as a beacon (light) of hope to all.  So when the storm ceases (stops), there is no change in our spiritual mindset.

Once again, it is inevitable that storms will arise in our lifetime. What to discern from this is choosing how you are going to deal with a storm regardless of what type (natural, social, financial, physical and mental).  Successful (positive) survival from any storm starts in the mental realm (internal conflict; spiritually or worldly).   By increasing our spirituality, we increase our faith by knowing that no storm is greater than our God.

Storms indeed will arise, and they come from various sources and forces: God, Satan, and Ourselves.

What to take from this chapter:

1. Storms are inevitable, so prepare your mind.

2. Understand the source of the storm and that it comes to test your mentality and spirituality.

3. You can create your storms by making poor choices.

# Chapter 22 – Your Mission – (Answer)

Your mission, if you choose to accept it? As I mentioned at the beginning of this book was from a popular TV show, and now movie series called, *"Mission: Impossible."* This question is important on so many levels because it refers to exercising one's free will that God has bestowed (given) upon all of humanity. By accepting a mission, one agrees to achieve a particular goal and to adapt to any circumstances that may arise in obtaining a favorable outcome. In essence, never lose sight of the objective or desired end-result, no matter what. It is our special assignment and reaching the goal supports a much bigger picture.

Recall the chapter that discussed the gift God has given us, which is our free will. Making choices that God would be proud of and indicative (telling) of what He expects. Now, what could be some of the choices we can make? Well, putting God's thoughts and practices first, then be of service toward others. Select a career that places you in a position of demand then build the knowledge and skill sets that others can rely upon. The wonderful thing about having free will and choices means God is not going to micro-manage (babysit).

A significant number of philosophers have questioned, why doesn't God take away man's free will so that we can all go to heaven? Well, God stands for truth and does not go back on what he has given or implemented (to do). However, He is a loving God who has longsuffering (tolerant) for humankind and demonstrates a will to reserve punishment toward us. But, when God does something, it is done. Just like when He gave man free will, He is not going to go back on His word.

Now, what exactly is the mission we need to accept or decline? It is to strive for heaven each day; live a Christ-like life; be ready and willing to serve others; discipleship in recruiting those who are lost; not waiver (change) when storms occur; put yourself in a career position that strengthens your values and principles from God; nurture (raise) our seeds (children) in God's laws. Further, express thanksgiving for the salvation provided by His Son, Jesus Christ.

Now, to do good deeds and exhibit (show) the behavior God wants you to, isn't enough according to Isaiah 64:6:

*"But we are all as an unclean thing, and all our righteousness are as filthy rags; and we all do fade as a leaf; and our iniquities, like the wind, have taken us away."*

The thing we all need to instill (put in) in our minds is found in John 3:16:

*"For God so loved the world that he gave his only begotten Son, that whosoever believeth in him should not perish, but have everlasting life."*

There is no other way to obtain this life's true rewards or the next life's rewards unless you believe in Christ the Son.  Plus, we can show our love and appreciation for Christ by mitigating (lessening) or eliminating (getting rid of) our amount of sin that circulates (mixes) with the rest of the world.

The goal is to return to the Lord as a pure being washed in His precious Son's Blood without having a spot or a wrinkle.  Indeed, there are some cute sayings created by man on how to get to heaven, for example:

*"First, make a right onto Believeth Boulevard. Keep going straight through the Green Light, which is Jesus Christ.  From there, you must turn onto the Bridge of Faith, which is over troubled water. When you get off the bridge, make a right turn and keep going straight.  You are on the Kings Highway-Heaven*

*bound! Keep going for three miles: One for the Father, One for the Son, and One for the Holy Ghost then exit off onto Grace Boulevard. From there, make a right turn on Gospel Lane. Keep going straight and then make another right on Prayer Road. As you go on your way, do not yield to the traffic on Temptation Avenue. Also, avoid Sin Street because it is a Dead End. Pass up Greed Avenue, Hypocrisy Street, Gossiping Road, and Backbiting Boulevard. You have to go down Long-suffering Lane, Persecution Boulevard, and Trials and Tribulations Avenue. But that's okay because Victory Boulevard is straight ahead! STAY THE COURSE." (DeA Foster and DWD Inspirational Pages).*

The positive words behind each of the direction in this inspirational thought are so truthful: Belief, Faith, Grace, Gospel, Prayer, Victory, Mercy, Peace, and Love. They have been bestowed upon us by Christ who shed His pure blood for all of humankind so that we can have fellowship with our Heavenly Father, now and in the world to come. Through His sacrifice, we inherit eternal life and blessings by just committing our thoughts to believe in Him. There is a verse spoken by Christ in His Sermon on the Mount found in Matthew 6:33:

*"But seek ye first the kingdom of God and his righteousness, and all these things shall be added unto you." (KJV)*

Just by believing and committing your thoughts to Christ and God's Kingdom, you automatically receive Love, Grace, Mercy, Peace, and Victory. To shorten the inspirational quote by DeA Foster and DWD, there is a much shorter and simpler quote from an anonymous author:

*"To get to heaven, all you have to do is turn right and keep straight…."*

As a current or future King or Queen (leader) to be an effective leader demands spiritual, mental, social, physical, and financial stamina; with demonstrated knowledge and work.

> *"Even so faith, if it hath not works, is dead, being alone. (James 2:17 KJV)*

Moreover, it is a personal sacrifice of yourself with an honest heart that seeks to serve people who have been put in your care. Your hearts desires should always be on the well-being of those you are a steward over. By doing so ensures your longevity as a leader and favor with God.

> *"He (Jesus) riseth from supper, and laid aside his garments, and took a towel, and girded himself. After that he poureth water into a bason, and began to wash the disciples' feet, and to wipe them with the towel wherewith he was girded." (John 13:4-5 KJV)*

Being an inspirational and effective leader is a state of mind that is always looking to God and being ready to serve (not waiting to be served). A key aspect of your development and growth is working on a personal constitution, which the contents and contexts of this book facilitate. Leaders remain in God's favor when they look to be mentored; then look for opportunities to mentor someone. That my Kings and Queens is your mission... if you shall choose to accept it?

Your mission, if you choose to accept it:
1. Strive for Heaven each day.
2. Live a Christ-like life.
3. Be ready and willing to serve.
4. Discipleship, to lead others to Christ.
5. Be strong in Christ when storms arise.
6. Obtain a career that exemplifies God and serves others.
7. Ready and willing to mentor the next generation in Christ and the salvation He provided for all who believe.

# Reading Suggestions

To improve your mind and polish your presentation skills; below is a list of reference material, books, and guides that are suggestions for developing one's persona. Further, some of the reading materials are great for building a stronger bond between a parent/mentor and child/mentee when reading together:

### Reference:
1. Bible (Read a Chapter or more each day of your life)

2. Nelson's or Harper's Bible Dictionary

3. Strong's Concordance (Handy when reading the Bible)

4. Webster Dictionary (Required for all courses and reading)

5. Black's Law Dictionary (Informative for legal matters)

6. Mosby's Medical Dictionary (Informative for medical matters)

7. Robert's Rules of Order (Guide on conducting meetings)

### Inspirational:
8. Purpose Driven Life by Rick Warren (Read as soon as possible)

9. Prayer's that Avail Much by Germaine Copeland (Read as soon as possible)

10. Every Man's Battle by Stephen Arterburn (14+ years old)

11. Joel Osteen's Series of Books and Study Guides (14+ years old)

12. The Secret by Yolanda Byrne (15+ years old)

13. Forgiving Forward by Bruce Hebel and Toni Hebel (Read as soon as possible)

14. Letter's to a Young Brother by Hill Harper (14+ years old)

**Brain Power:**
15. Barron's 1100 Words You Need To Know (14+ years old)

16. Grammar and Writer's Guide (14+ years)

17. How to Solve Mathematical Word Problems (14+ years old)

18. Learn the origins of Latin and Greek Words (14+ years old)

19. Speed Reading Book (16+ years old)

20. Improve Your Memory (16+ years old)

21. Logic Puzzles and Games (14+ years old)

22. IQ Quizzes and Tests (14+ years old)

23. How to Play Chess (8+ years old)

24. Where There's A Will, There's An A (12+ years old)

**Relationships:**
25. How to Win Friends and Influence Others by Dale Carnegie (16+ years old)

26. Ed Young's Series of Books and Study Guides (14+ years old)

27. The Art of War by Sun Tzu (18+ years old)

28. The Art of Peace by Sun Tzu (18+ years old)

**Scholastic:**
29. ACT (American College Test) prep books (14+ years old)

30. SAT (Scholastic Assessment Test) prep books (14+ years old)

31. LSAT (Law School Admissions Test) prep books (Read the third year in college or after)

32. GMAT (Graduate Management Admissions Test/GRE (Graduate Record Exam) prep books (Read the third year in college or after)

33. MCAT (Medical College Admissions Test) prep books (Read the third year in college or after)

34. Military Aptitude (Officer & Enlisted) ASVAB (16+ years old)

**Self Help:**
35. Any type, it helps to build a relationship when working together

36. Administering First Aid or EMT (Read at 10+ years old, builds on relationships)

37. Self-Help Automotive Guides (Read at 12+ years old, building on relationships)

38. Self -Help Home Improvements (Electrical and Plumbing – 10+ years old, builds on relationships)

**Financial:**
39. Real Estate Investment (16+ years old)

40. Careers and Salary Guide (14+ years old)

41. Rich Dad Poor Dad by Robert Kiyosaki (17+ years old)

42. The Total Money Makeover by Dave Ramsey (21+ years old)

The above are suggested books that are quick help guides to help build your knowledge base. However, the key is taking the time to review the material on more than one occasion. There is an old common saying, *"If you don't use what you know, you lose it…."* Nonetheless, these are only recommendations and in no way should you be limited by what is on this list. It only serves as a suggestion for future reading when you're bored, looking to bond with one another, or improve on one's self.

# About the Author

T.J. Faulk is a native of Long Island, NY. He was raised in a Christian home by his father and mother, Deacon and Deaconess Faulk who are both retired since 2003 and married for over 60 years. T.J. Faulk received Christ at an early age in 1978 at First Baptist Church of Wyandanch, NY under the leadership of Pastor Moses Robinson Jr.

T.J. Faulk completed his Doctorate of Information Technology in 2023 and Masters of Arts Political Science in 1995 from Long Island University (C.W. Post Campus). Also, he holds degrees in Sociology/Communication and Criminal Justice. To augment his formal education he acquired multiple technical certifications germane to cyber-security where he currently holds a Vice President position in Information Security Governance at a growing financial institution.

His past industry experience is diverse with exposure in various disciplines: Media and Communication, Defense Contract, Insurance, and Legal, Information Technology, and Financial. Recently, T.J. Faulk retired from the Air National Guard (USAF-Reserve) with over 27 years of service at the rank of Lt. Colonel.

While in the Military and Defense Contract industry T.J. Faulk was mentored by Senior Leadership and Staff, while at the same time mentoring recruits and subordinates. Presently, T.J. Faulk is an active mentor with Cobb and Douglas County School systems, the Non-profit mentoring group called, S.T.E.E.L. (Strong Tenacious Empowering Educated Leaders) Mentoring.

T. J. Faulk has an unending passion for mentoring. As a recent retiree from the military reserves, in his free time, he seeks opportunities to help establish Christian based mentoring programs. To show his dedication a portion of the proceeds from the sale of this book is going to support specific mentoring programs.

# Chess Pieces on the Cover

**Front Cover:**

The Blue Glass King and Queen Chess pieces represent a cool and calm appeal that is similar to looking at the sky and sea. The color Blue represents stability and depth. *It symbolizes trust, loyalty, wisdom, confidence, intelligence, faith, truth, and heaven. Blue is considered beneficial to the mind and body.* The author aspires to reach readers holding one or more of the symbolic characteristics. (www.color-wheel-pro.com).

Scriptures related to Blue - Exodus 24:10, 25:3, 38:18, Numbers 4:6 - 12, 2 Chronicles 2:7, Ezekiel 1:26, Esther 1:6, Ezekiel 23:6, Jeremiah 10:9, Ezekiel 27:7, 24, Exodus 28:6, 8, 13, 31, Numbers 15:38 - 40, Esther 8:15.

**Back Cover:**

The Purple Glass King and Queen Chess pieces represent the color purple and is symbolic of royalty, nobility, luxury, power, and ambition. *Purple also represents wealth, extravagance, creativity, wisdom, dignity, grandeur, devotion, peace, pride, mystery, independence, and magic.* As each reader completes this book, may you be blessed with a personal mental transformation that lets you know you are and will always be Royalty. (www.bourncreative.com).

Scriptures related to Purple - Judges 8:26, Esther 8:15 Exodus 28:5, Ezekiel 27:7, Proverbs 31:22, Song of Solomon 3:10, 7:5, Luke 16:19, Acts 16:14, Revelation 17:4, 18:12, 16.

Artistic Creativity – Keith Saunders at Marion Designs

# References and Credits

**Movie and Television:**

1. Mission: Impossible by Bruce Geller. Desilu Productions & Paramount Television. 1966 to 1973 Television Series.

2. The Best of Eddie Murphy: Saturday Night Live Director Andy Breckman. Eddie Murphy Television and NBC Productions. 1989 Video.

3. Vampire in Brooklyn Director Wes Craven. Eddie Murphy Productions and Paramount Pictures. 1995 Movie

4. Love & Basketball Director Gina Prince-Byethewood. 40 Acres and a Mule Filmworks. 2000 Movie.

5. Where There's A Will, There's An "A" by Professor Claude Olney. American Educational Publishers.1986 DVD

**Books:**

6. Dante Alighieri, 1265-1321. The Divine Comedy of Dante Alighieri : Inferno, Purgatory, Paradise. New York: The Union Library Association, 1935. Print.

7. Harper, Hill, 2006. Letters to a Young Brother: Manifest Your Destiny. New York: Published by Penguin Group, 2006. Paperback.

8. Bolander, Donald 1969 & 1972. Instant Quotation Dictionary. New York: Published by Dell Publishing Group Inc.1990 Paperback

9. Manser, Martin 2001. Christian Quotations. Louisville KY. Published by Westminster John Knox Press. 2001 Printed

10. Hebel, Bruce & Toni. 2011. Forgiveness Forward. Fayetteville GA, Publisher: ReGenerating Life Press. 2011 Paperback

11. Ramsey, Dave. 2003. The Total Money Makeover. Publishing by Thomas Nelson Publishers. 2003 Printed

12. Kiyosaki, Robert & Lechter, Sharon. 1997. Rich Dad Poor Dad. Publishing by Moses & Violet Karma Publishers Inc. 1997. Printed

13. Lindlar, Victor. 1942. You Are What You Eat. Published by National Nutrition Society, Inc. 1942 Paperback.

14. Bromberg, Murray. 1971 1100 Words You Need to Know Published by Barron's Educational Series Inc. 1993 Paperback

15. Jost, David. 1993.The American Heritage College Dictionary Third Edition published by Houghton Mifflin Company Boston and New York. 1993 Print

16. Youngblood, R.F. 1995, 1986 Nelson's Bible Dictionary by Thomas Nelson Publishers1995, 1986 Print

**Internet References:**

17. https://bible.org/

18. https://www.biblegateway.com/

19. voiceoftruthblog.com/reading-through-leviticus

20. www.lifehopeandtruth.com

21. https://www.careeronestop.org/

22. www.careers.org/research

23. https://www.psychologytoday.com/

24. https://childdevelopmentinfo.com/child-development/erickson

25. www.vtaide.com/gleanings/Kings-of-Israel/kings.html

26. https://www.britannica.com/

27. www.color-wheel-pro.com

28. www.bourncreative.com

29. https://www.thoughtco.com/prophecies-of-jesus-fulfilled

30. http://www.deadlysins.com/

**Quote Credits:**

Albert Camus
Thomas Hardy
Maya Angelo
Confuscious
DeA Foster and DWD Inspirational
Martin Luther King Jr.
Malcolm X
Alan Redpath

www.ingramcontent.com/pod-product-compliance
Lightning Source LLC
LaVergne TN
LVHW051558070426
835507LV00021B/2647